What is Inktober?

It's a month long drawing challenge that was created by **Jake Parker** in 2009. Inktober enabled him to improve his inking skills and since then it has become a worldwide event. The fact that other artists started using the techniques invented by Jake, has made Inktober a phenomenon. Now, each year in the month of October, more and more artists have participated by showing off their skills. The whole idea is to do a single traditional ink drawing for each day of the month and share it on social media for other artists to enjoy and become inspired.

If you are looking for inspiration, or having difficulty on figuring out what to draw, don't worry. You can go to: **inktober.com** for a prompt list. This list will have a word that will be assigned for each day of the month. You can use the prompts as a guide to help you with your work.

START DRAWING AND DISPLAYING YOUR TALENTS

Inktober rules:

1. Draw with ink *(sketch in pencil first, if you like)*
2. Upload your work to any social media platform
3. Use the hash tags **#inktober #inktober2017** *(or the current year)*

If you need help inking, or just trying to figure out what supplies to use visit: **inktober.com**

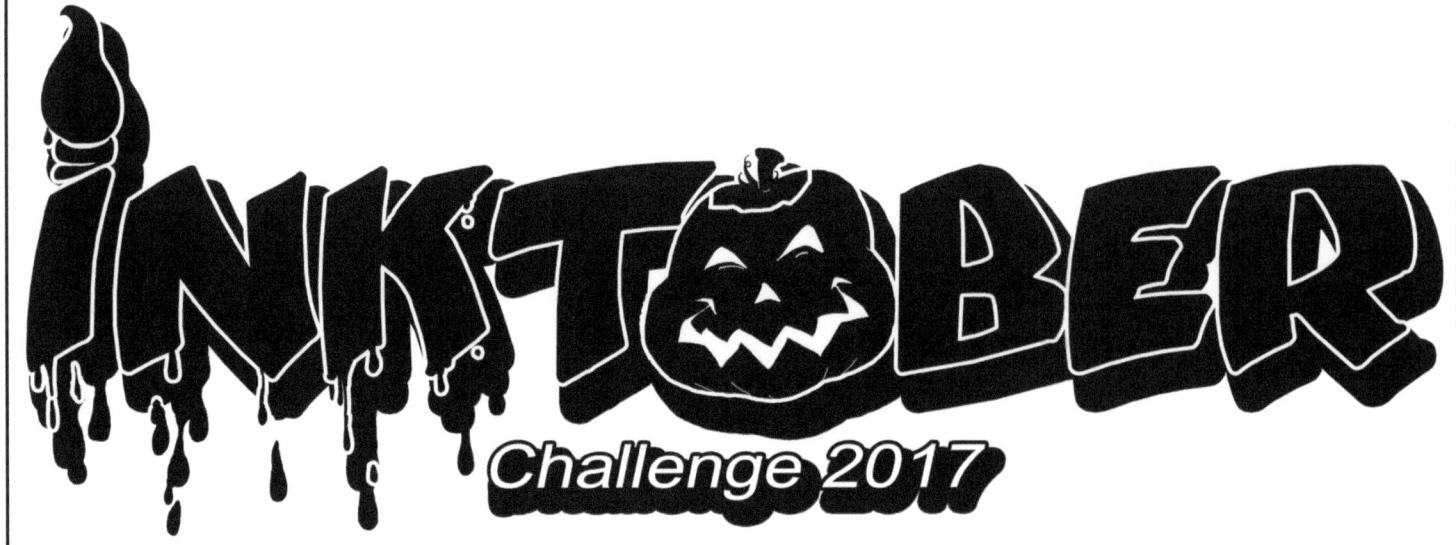

Official Prompt List

1. Swift
2. Divided
3. Poison
4. Underwater
5. Long
6. Sword
7. Shy
8. Crooked
9. Screech
10. Gigantic
11. Run
12. Shattered
13. Teeming
14. Fierce
15. Mysterious
16. Fat
17. Graceful
18. Filthy
19. Cloud
20. Deep
21. Furious
22. Trail
23. Juicy
24. Blind
25. Ship
26. Squeak
27. Climb
28. Fall
29. United
30. Found
31. Mask

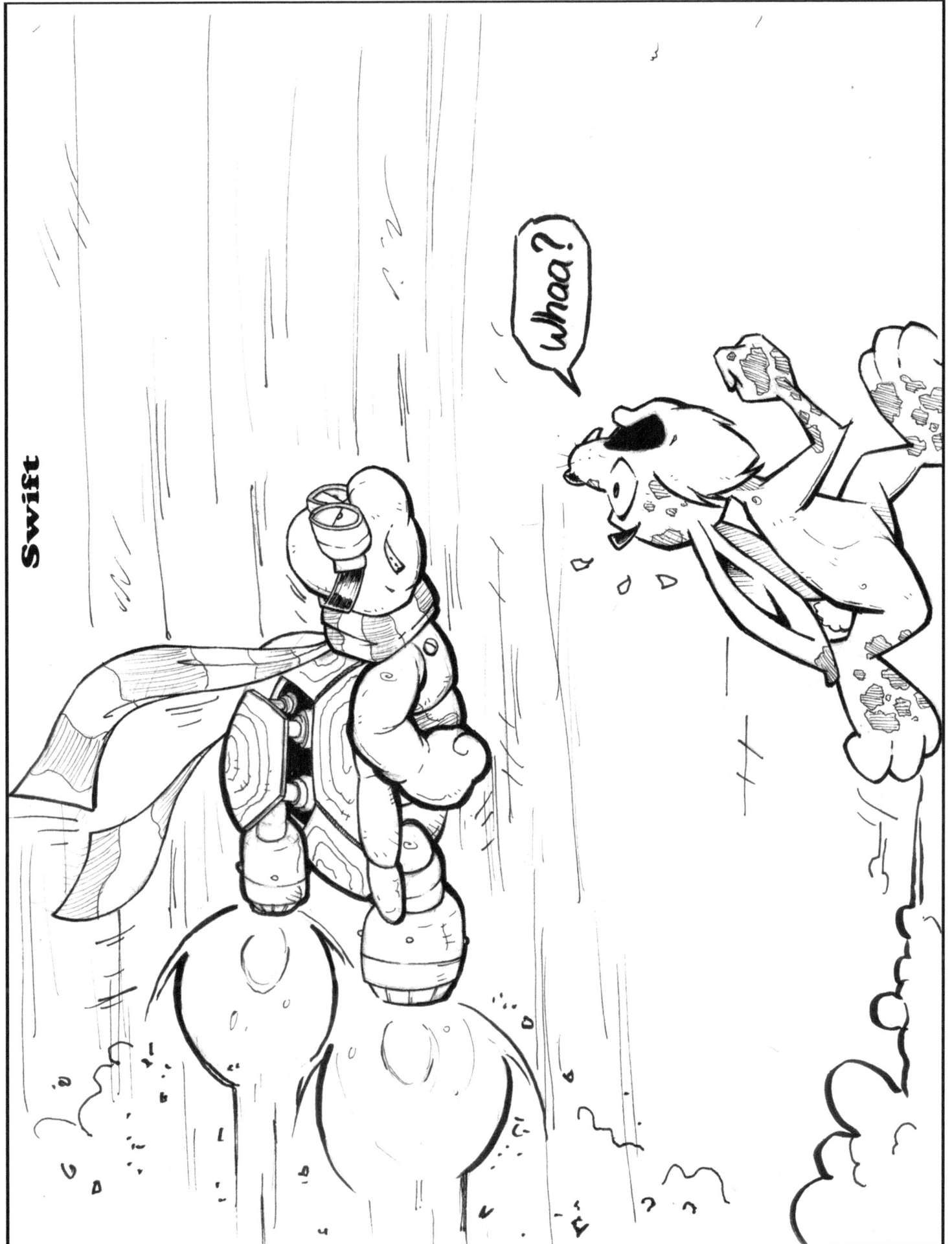

Divided

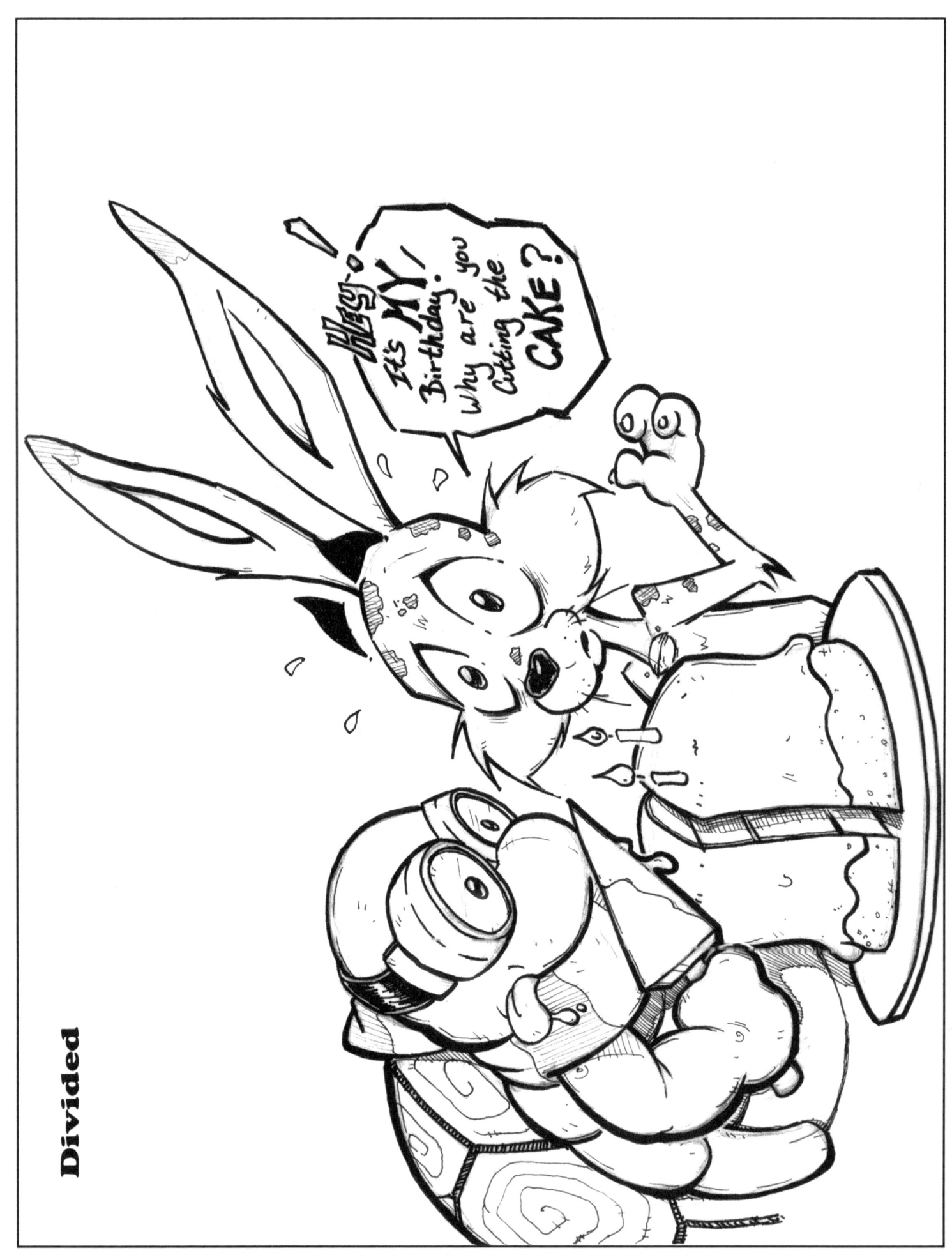

Poison

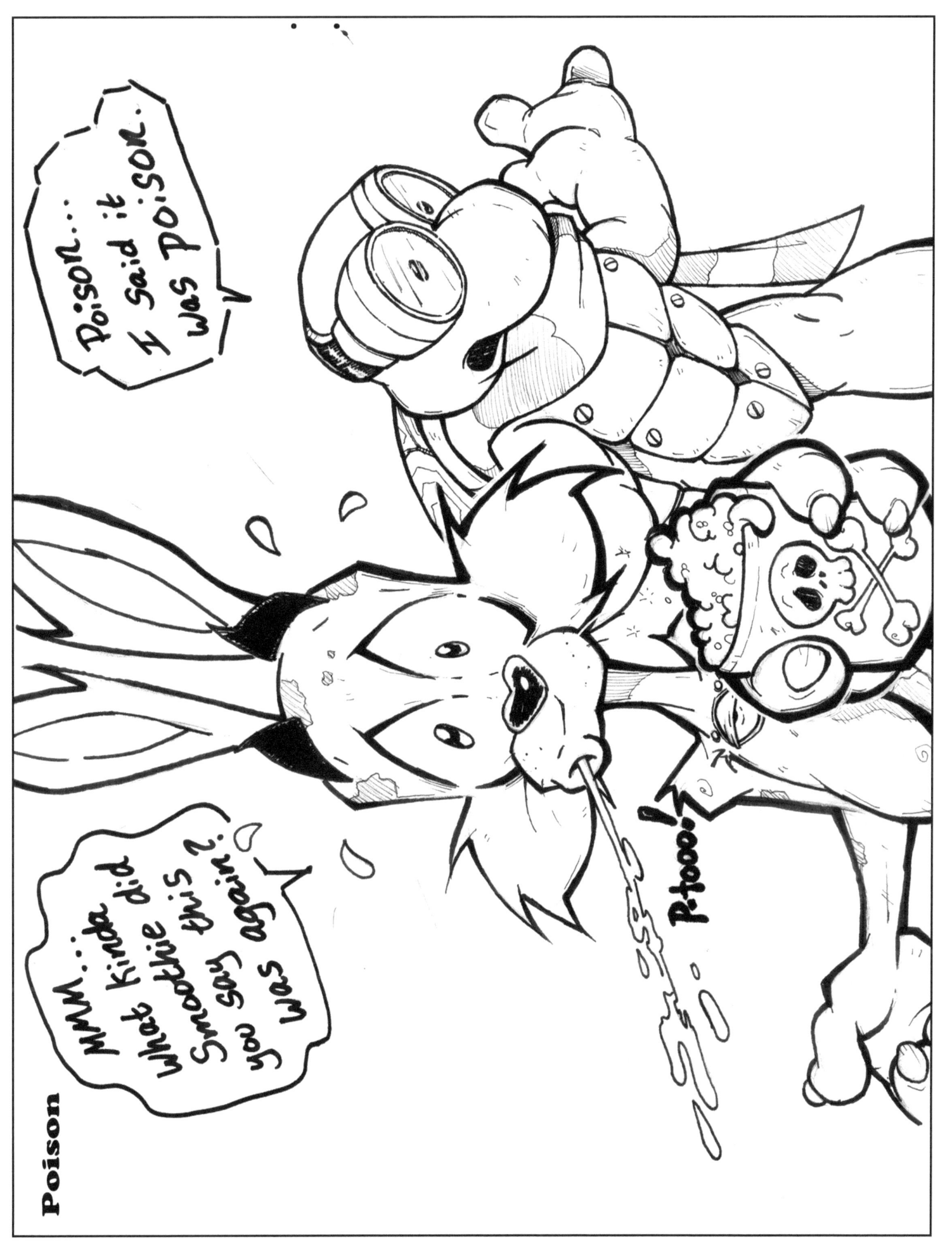

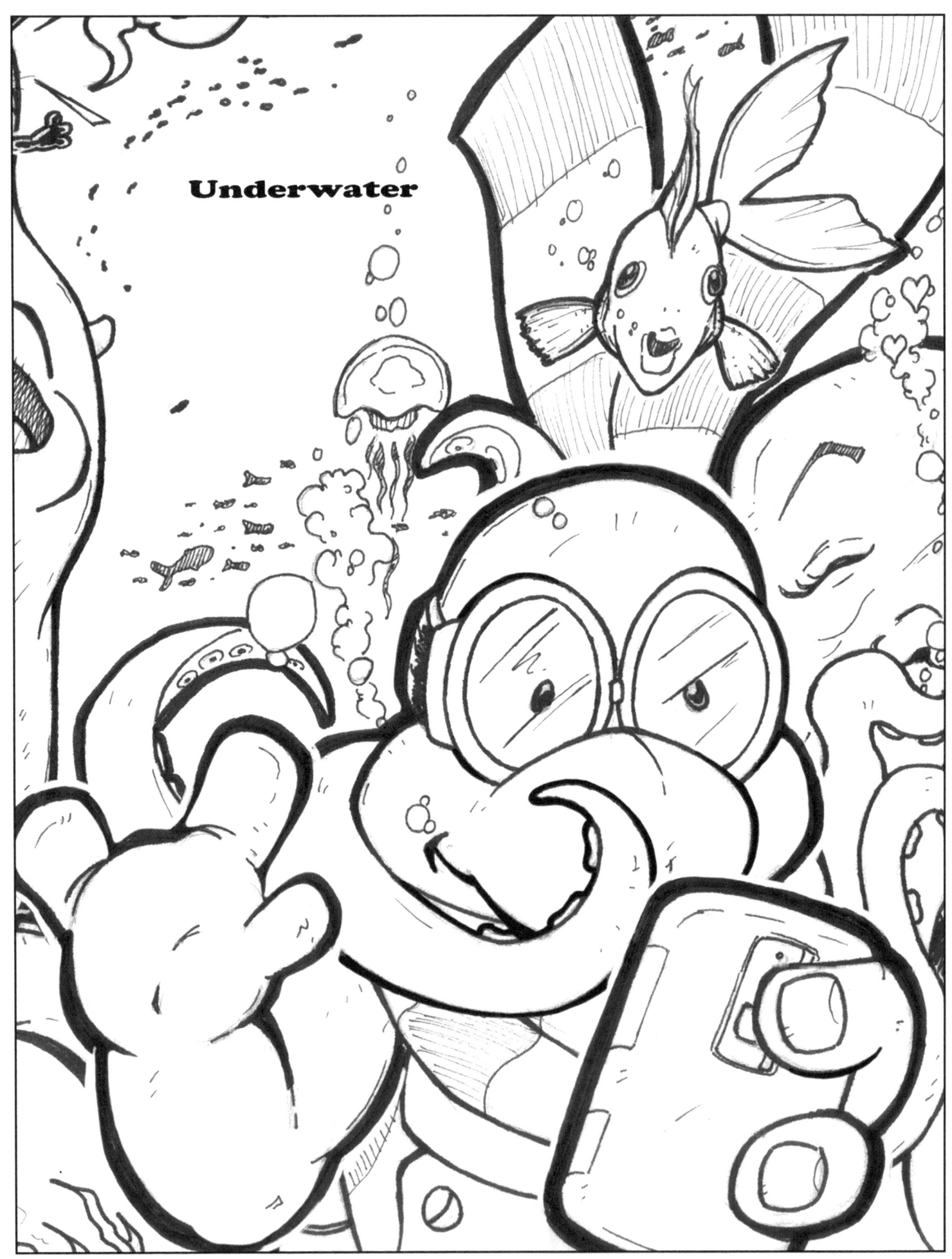

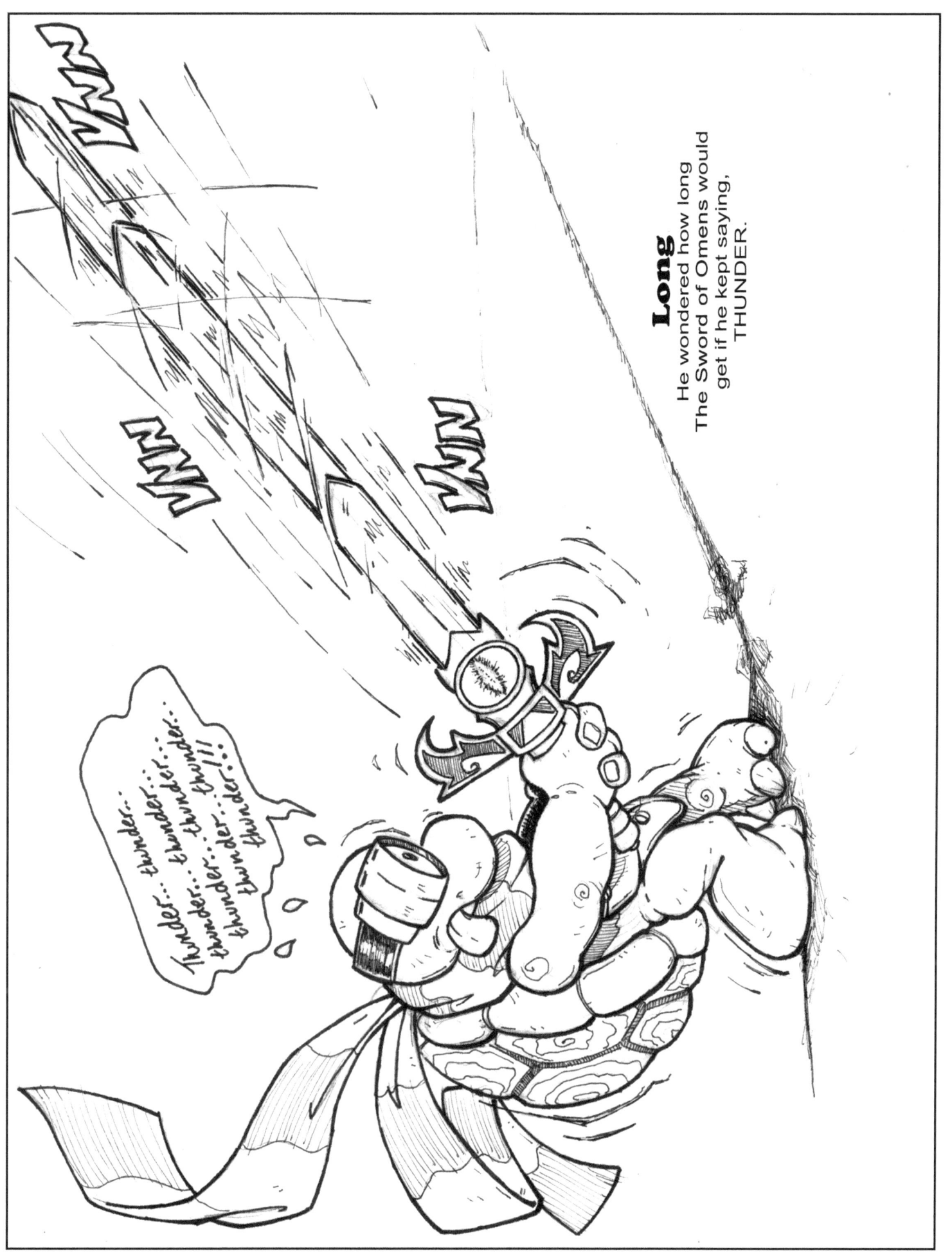

Long

He wondered how long The Sword of Omens would get if he kept saying, THUNDER.

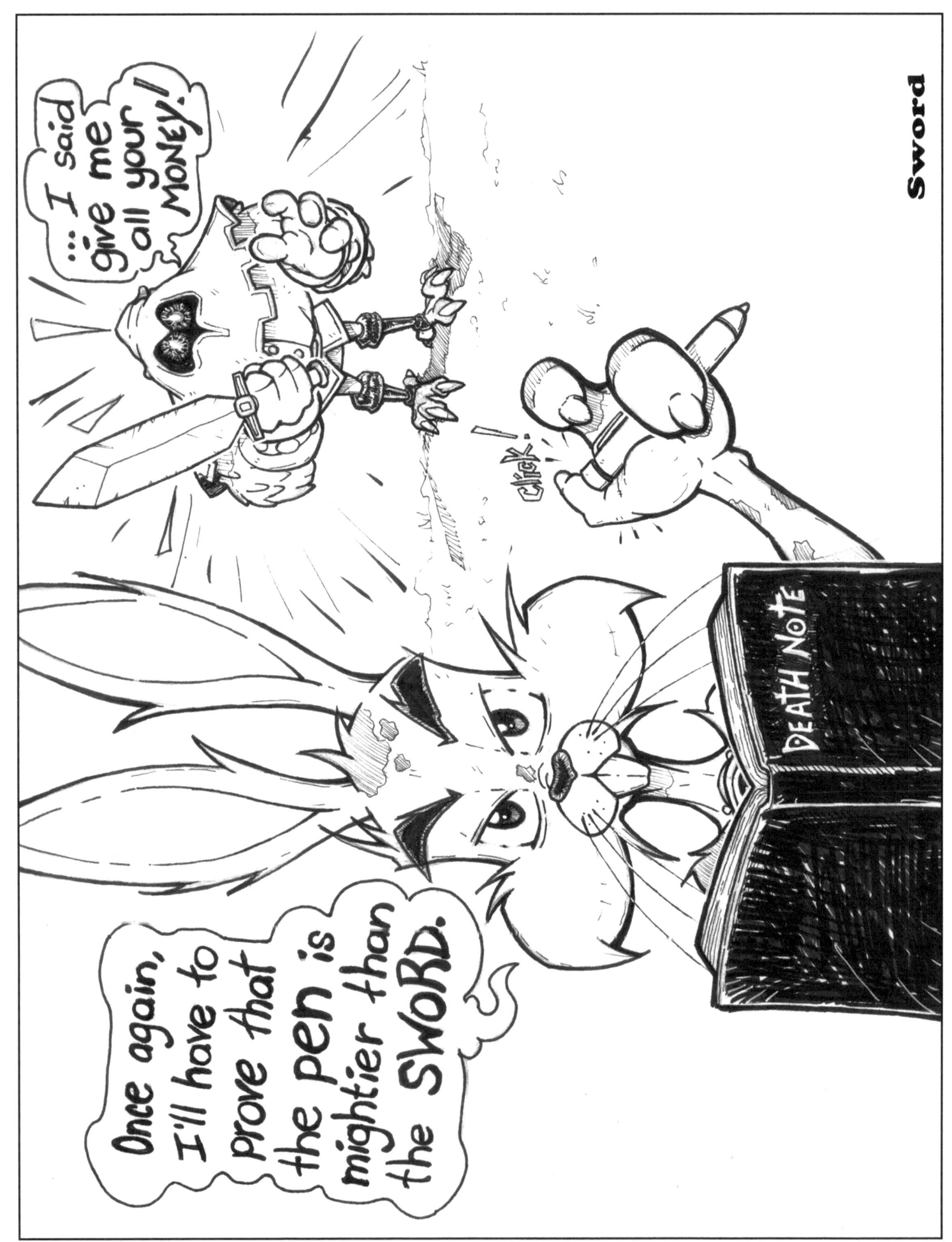

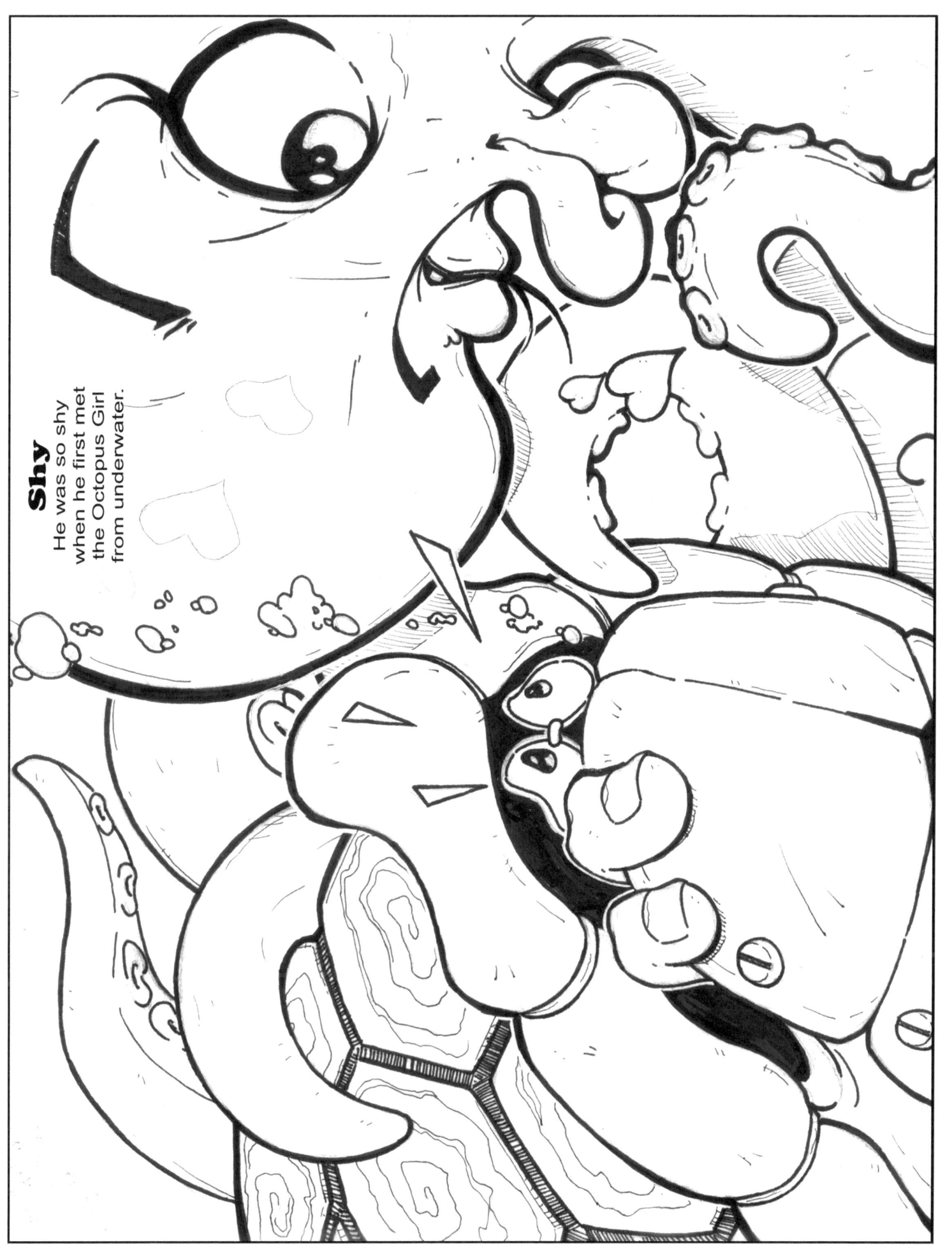

Crooked

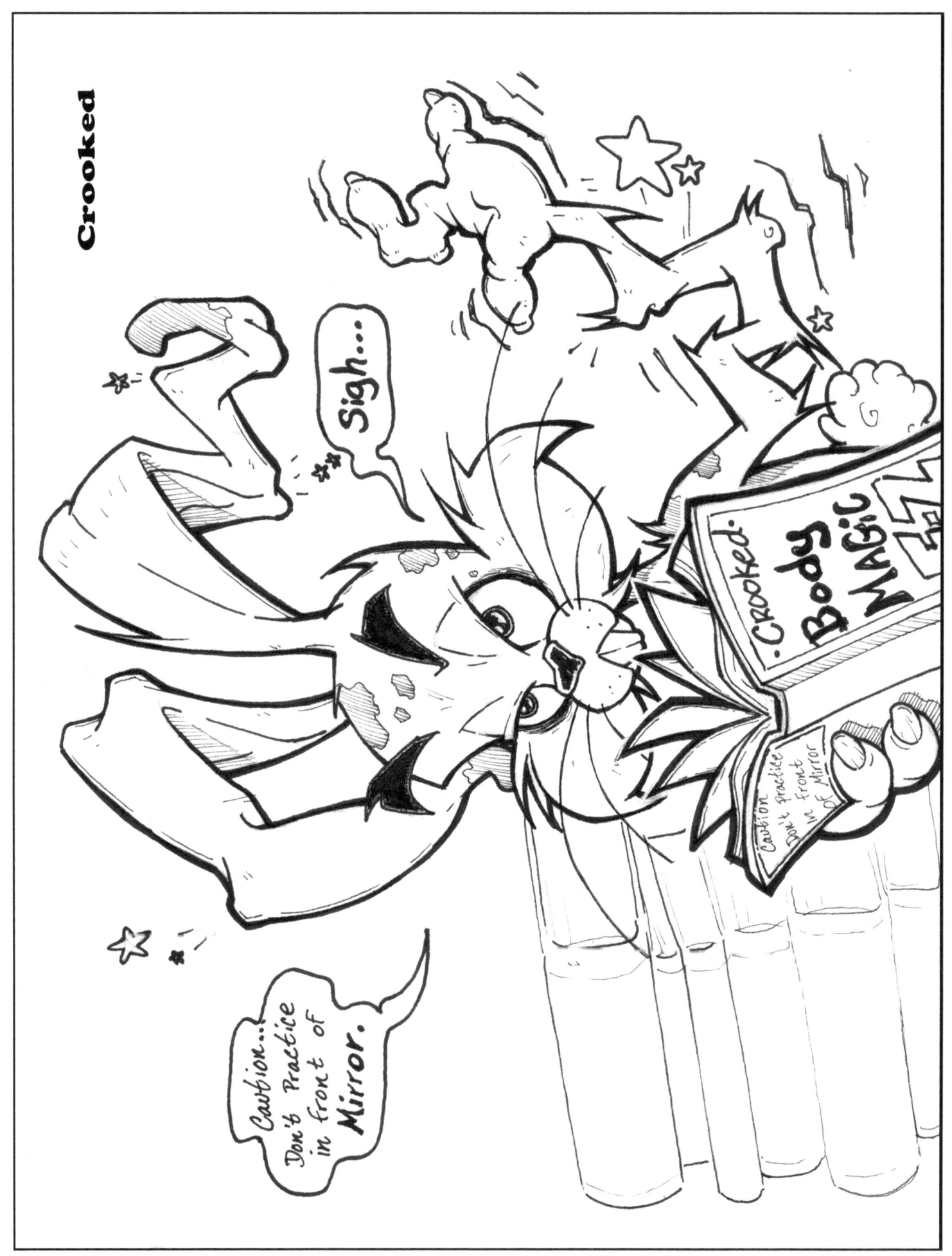

Screech

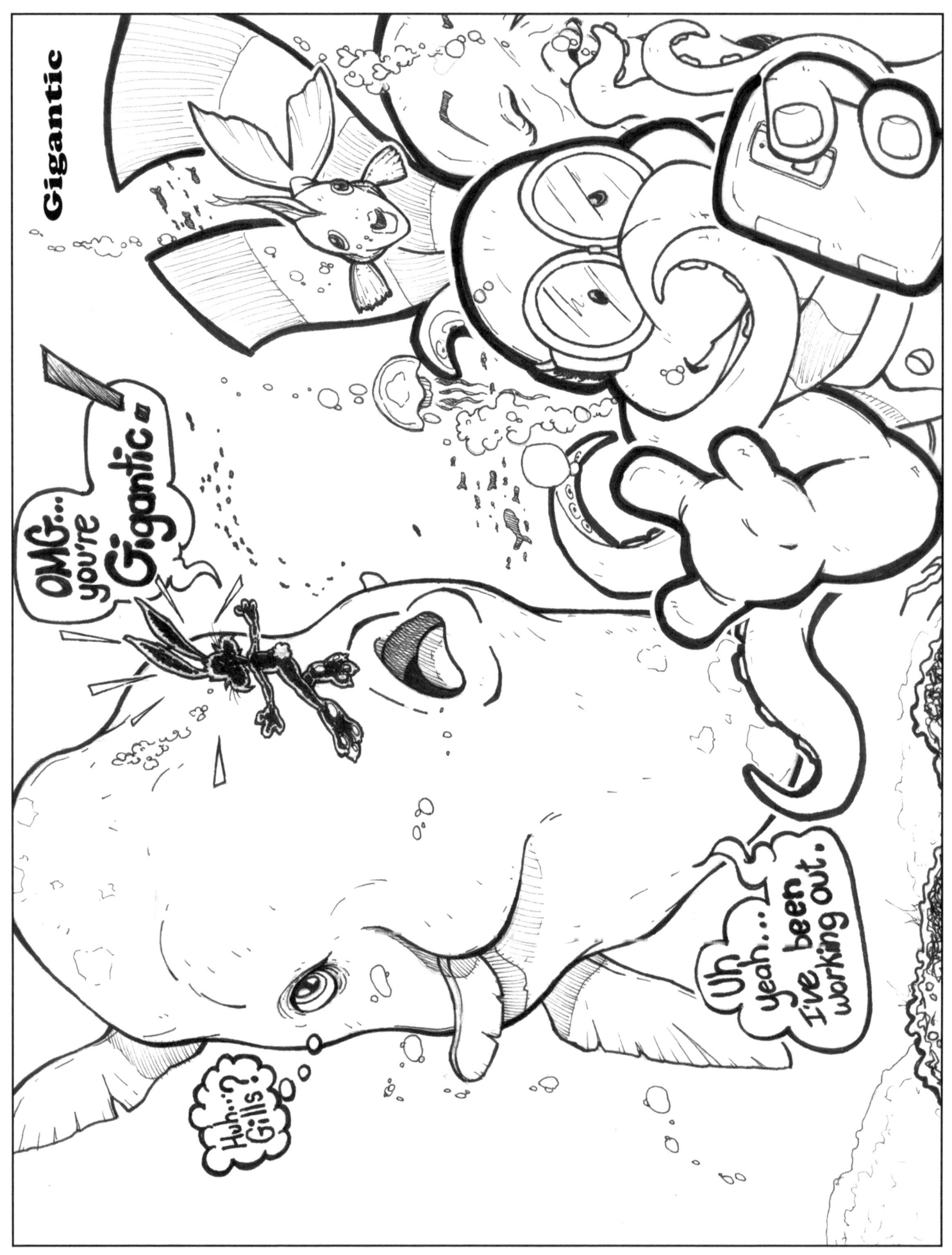

Run

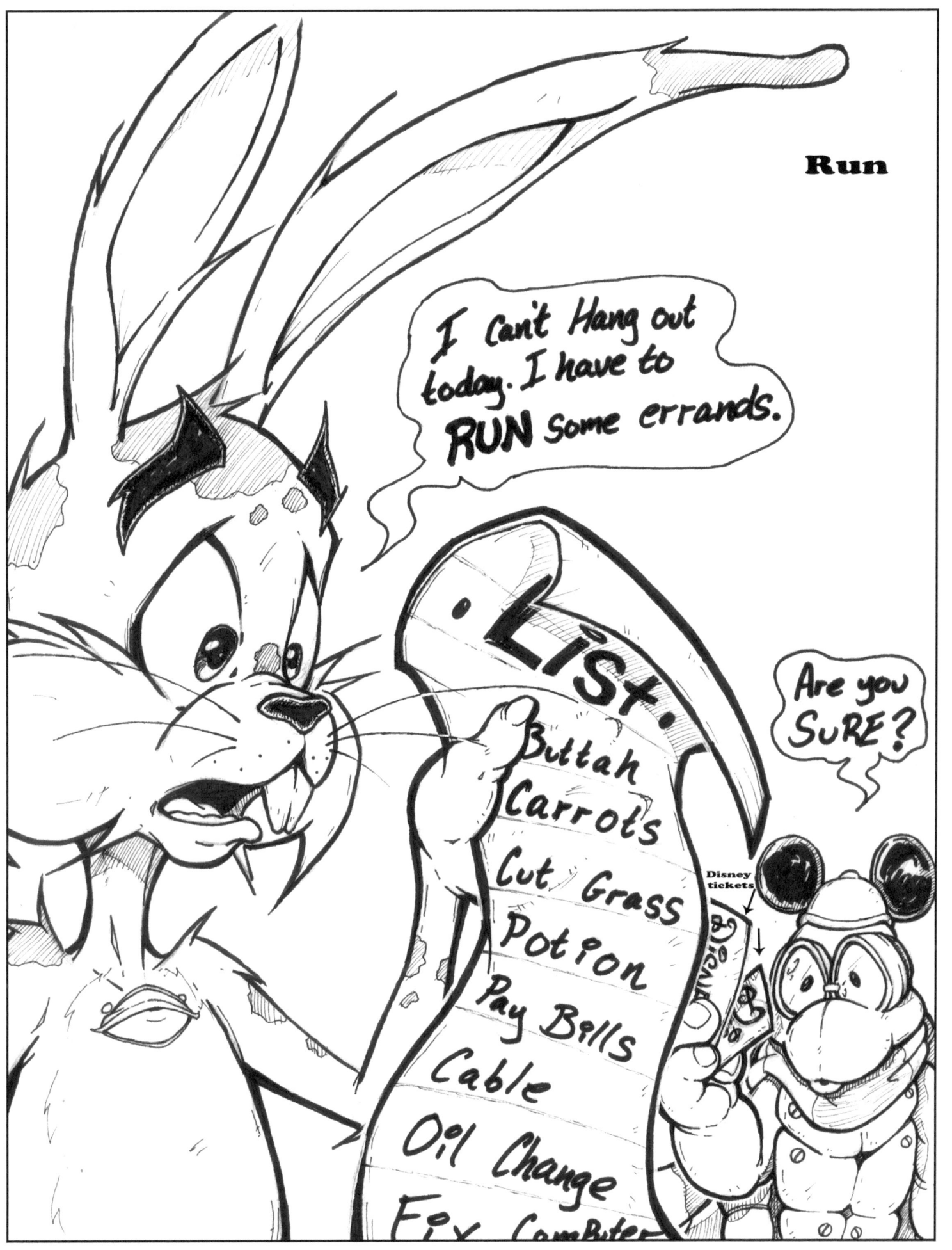

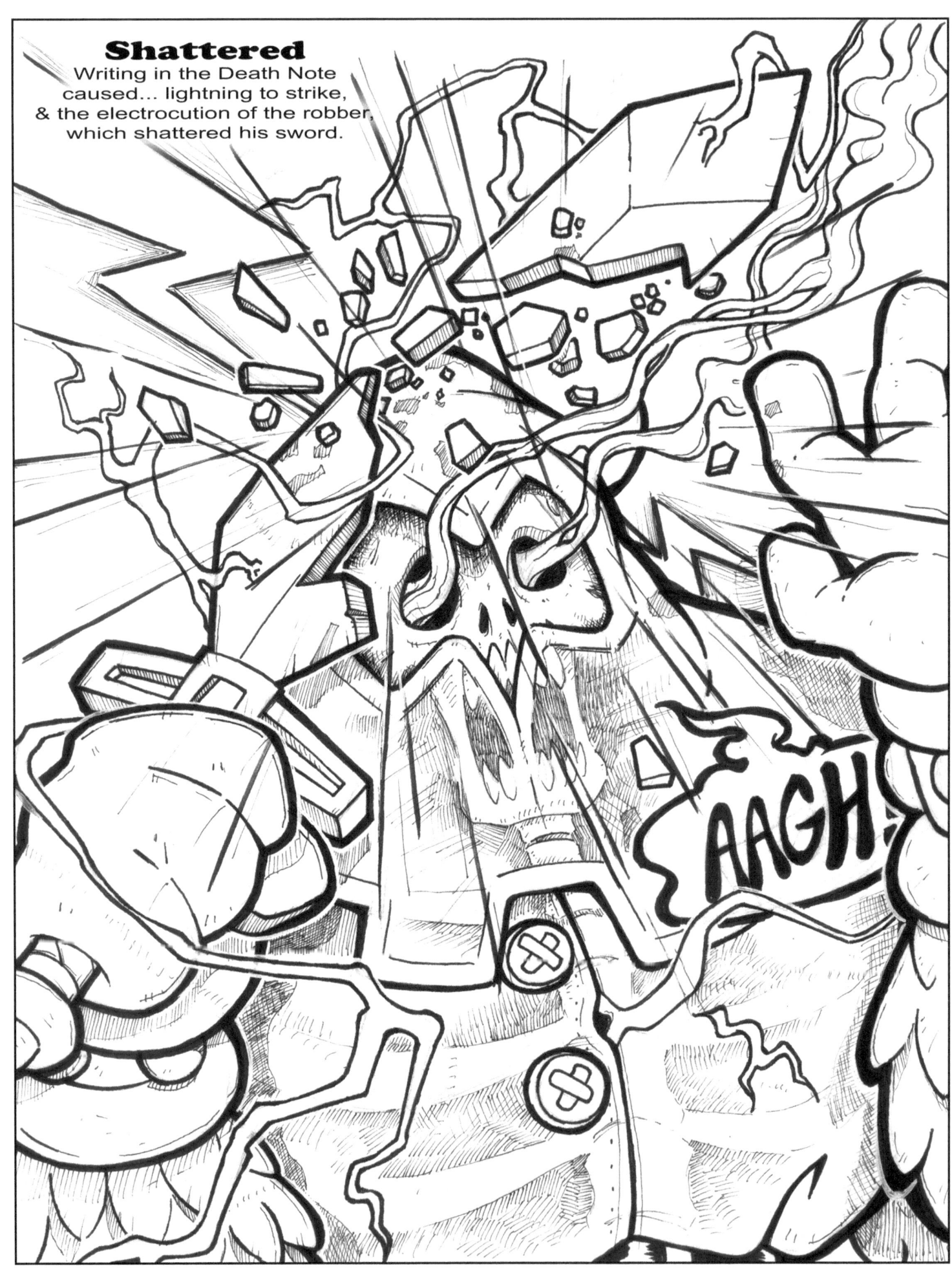

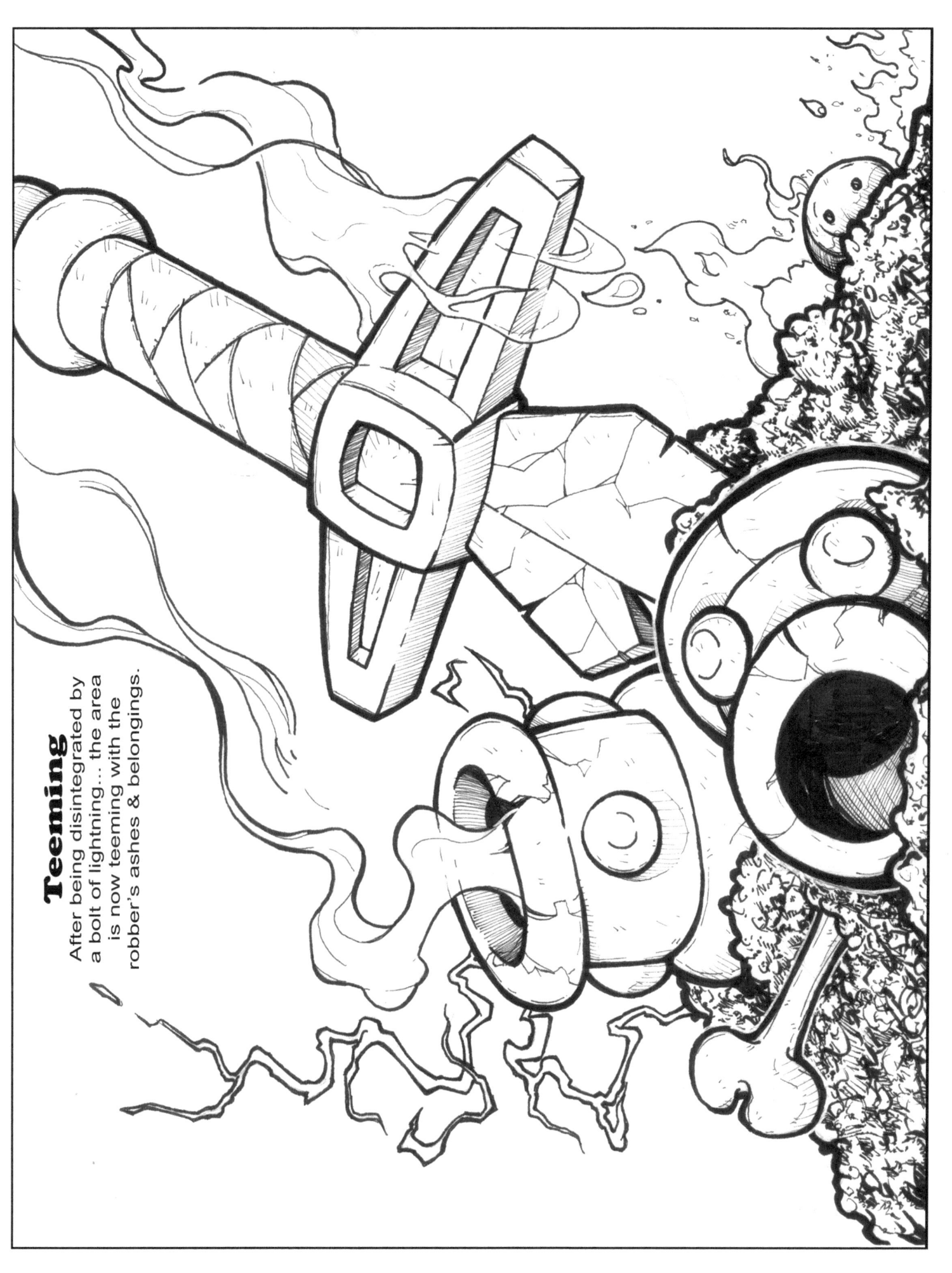

Teeming

After being disintegrated by a bolt of lightning... the area is now teeming with the robber's ashes & belongings.

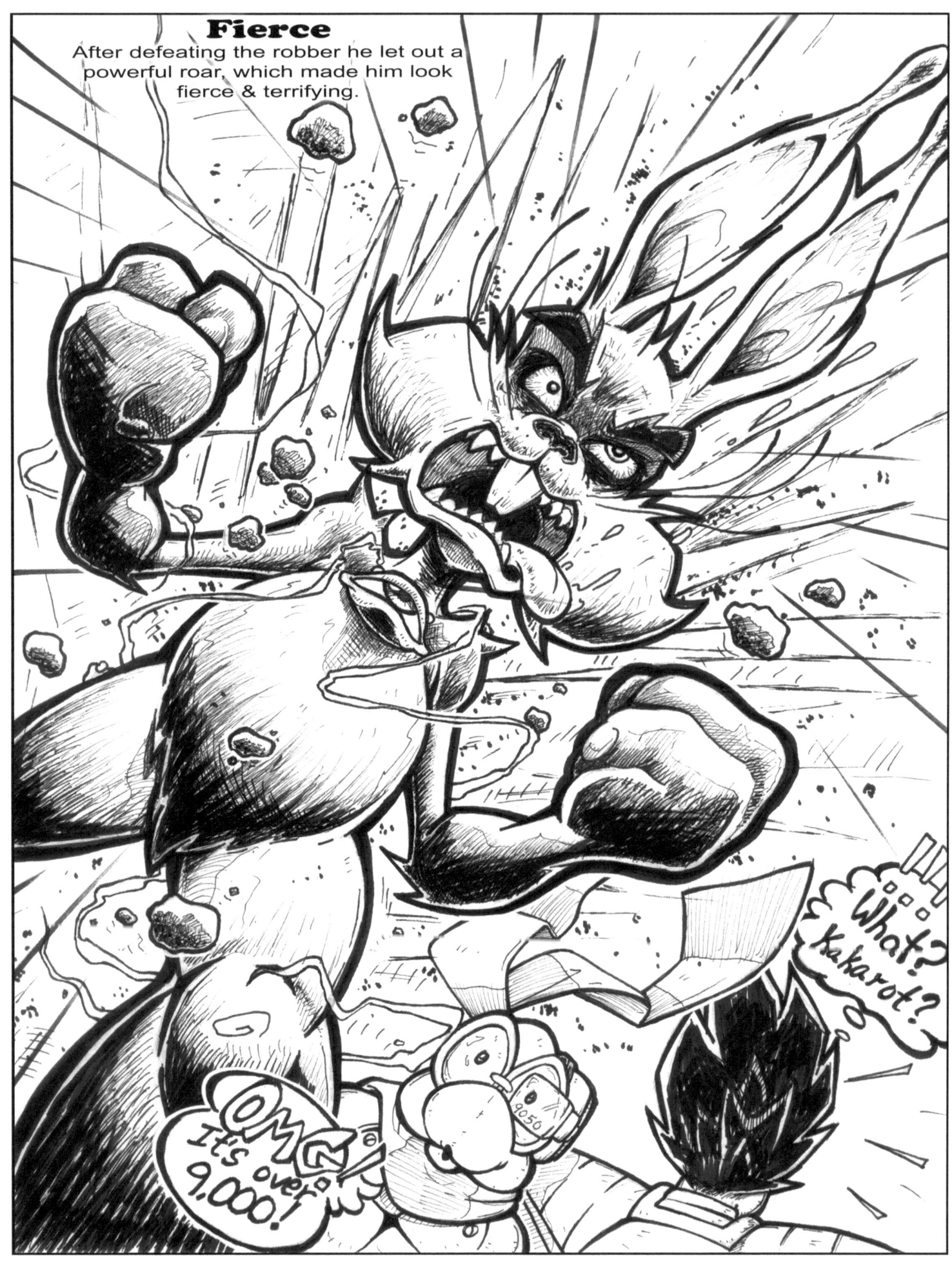

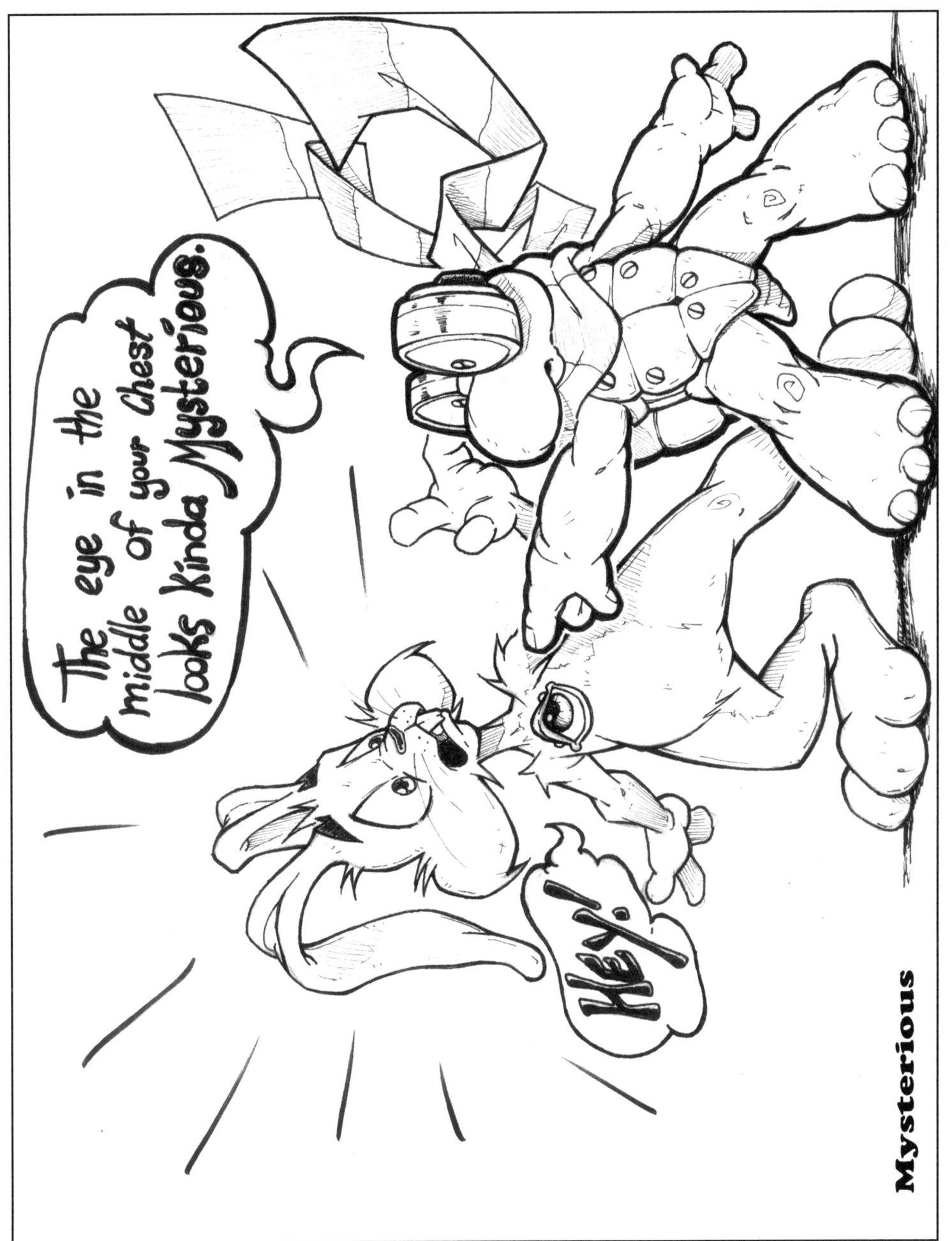

Mysterious

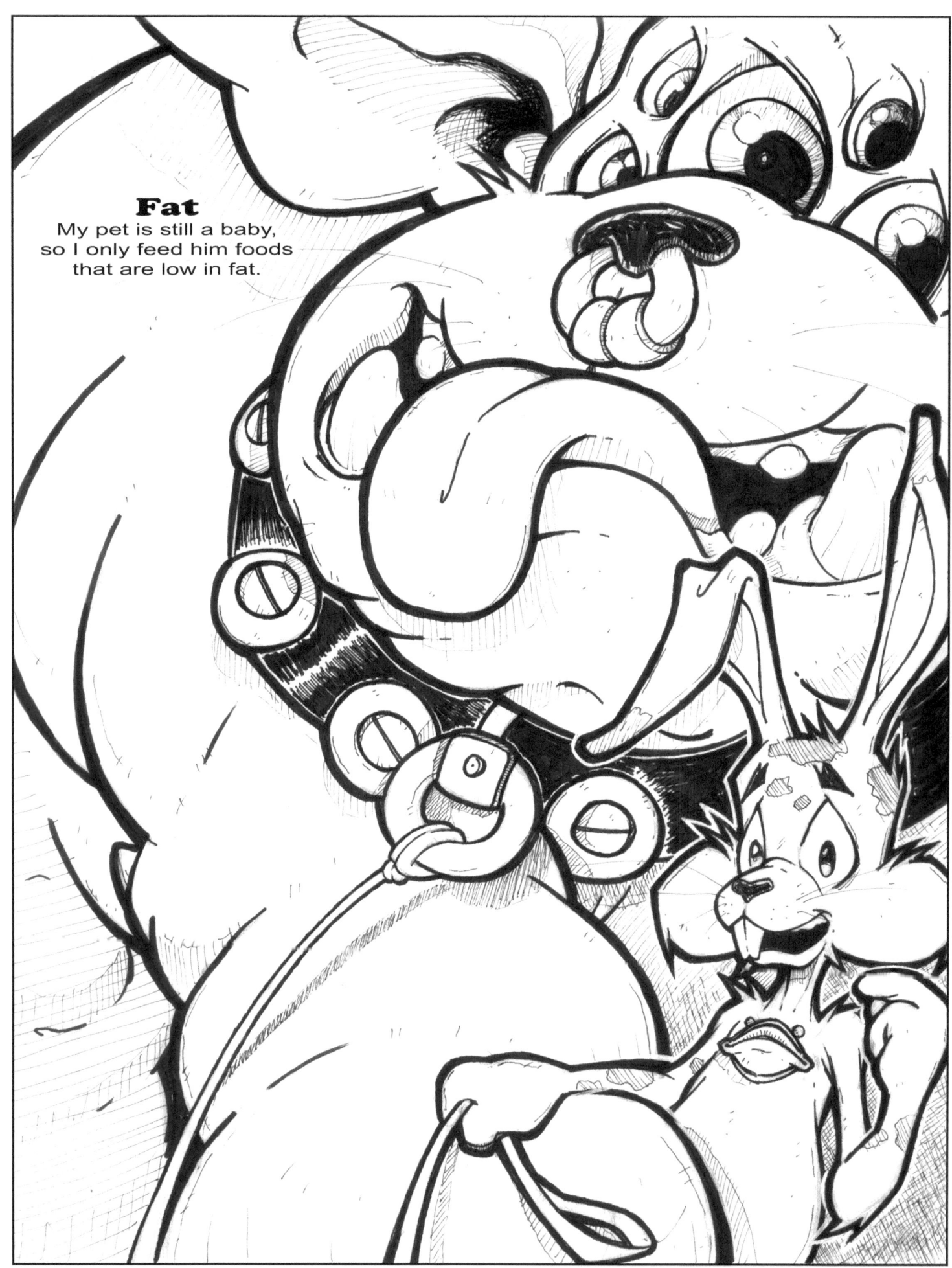

Fat
My pet is still a baby, so I only feed him foods that are low in fat.

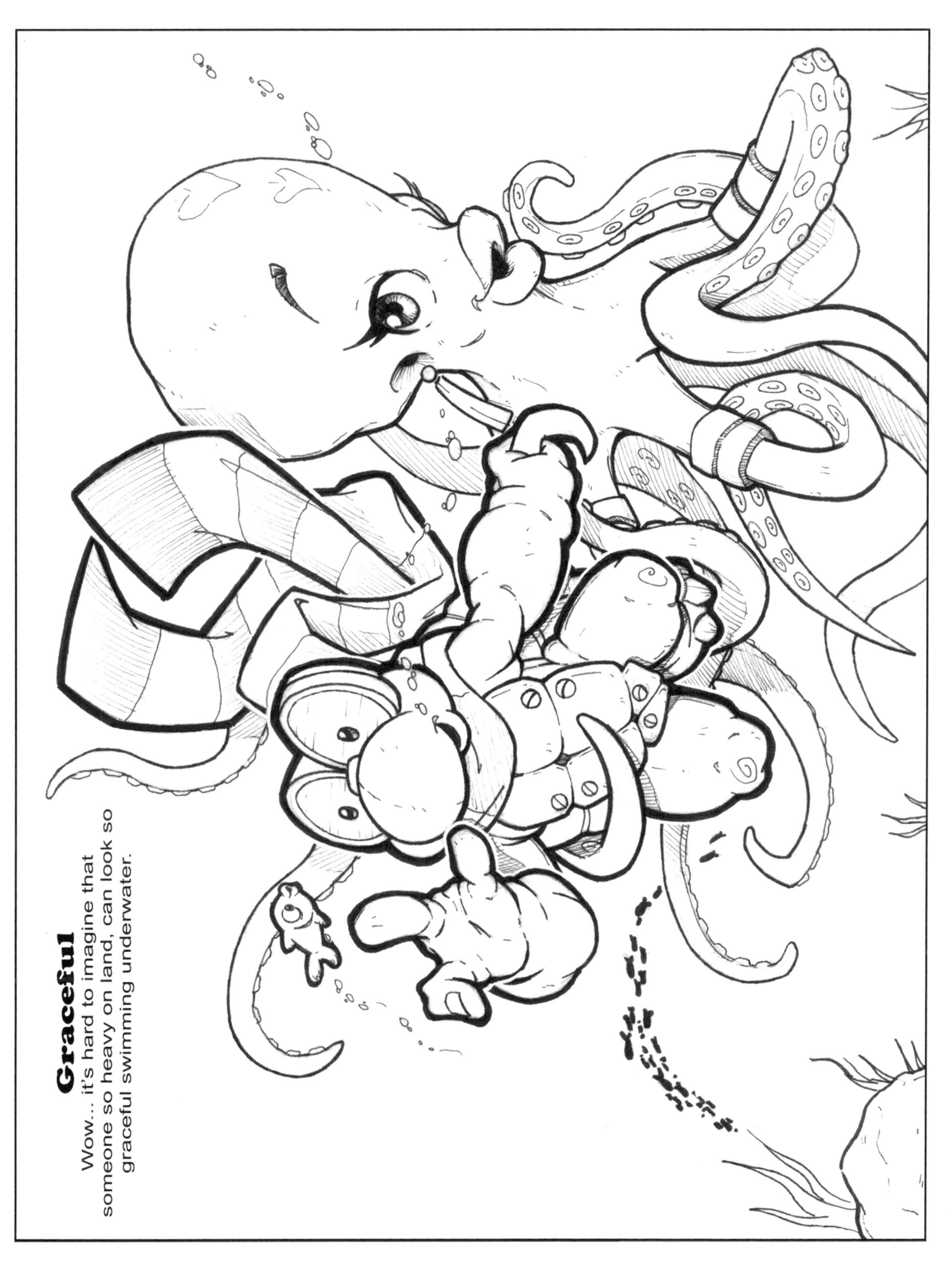

Graceful

Wow... it's hard to imagine that someone so heavy on land, can look so graceful swimming underwater.

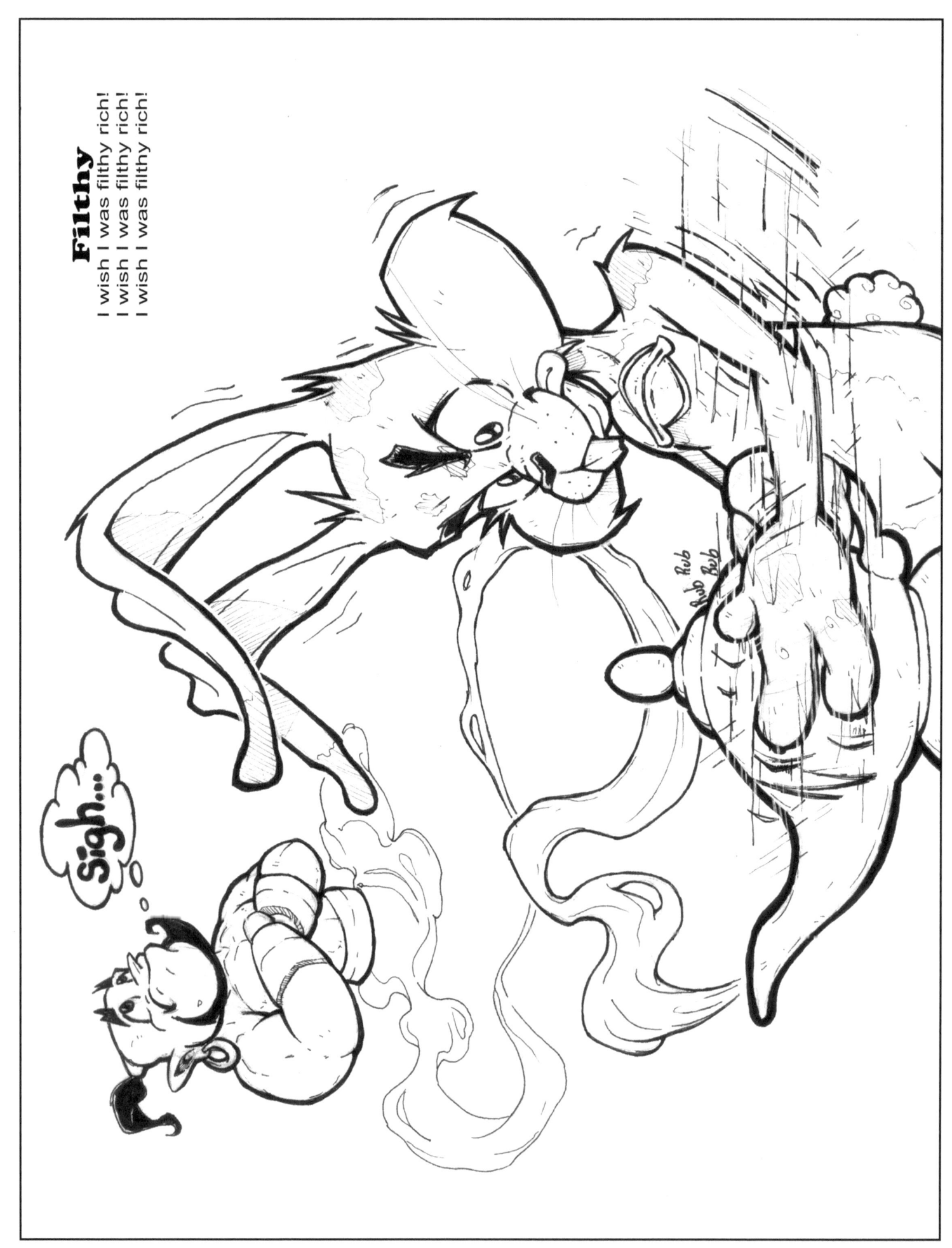

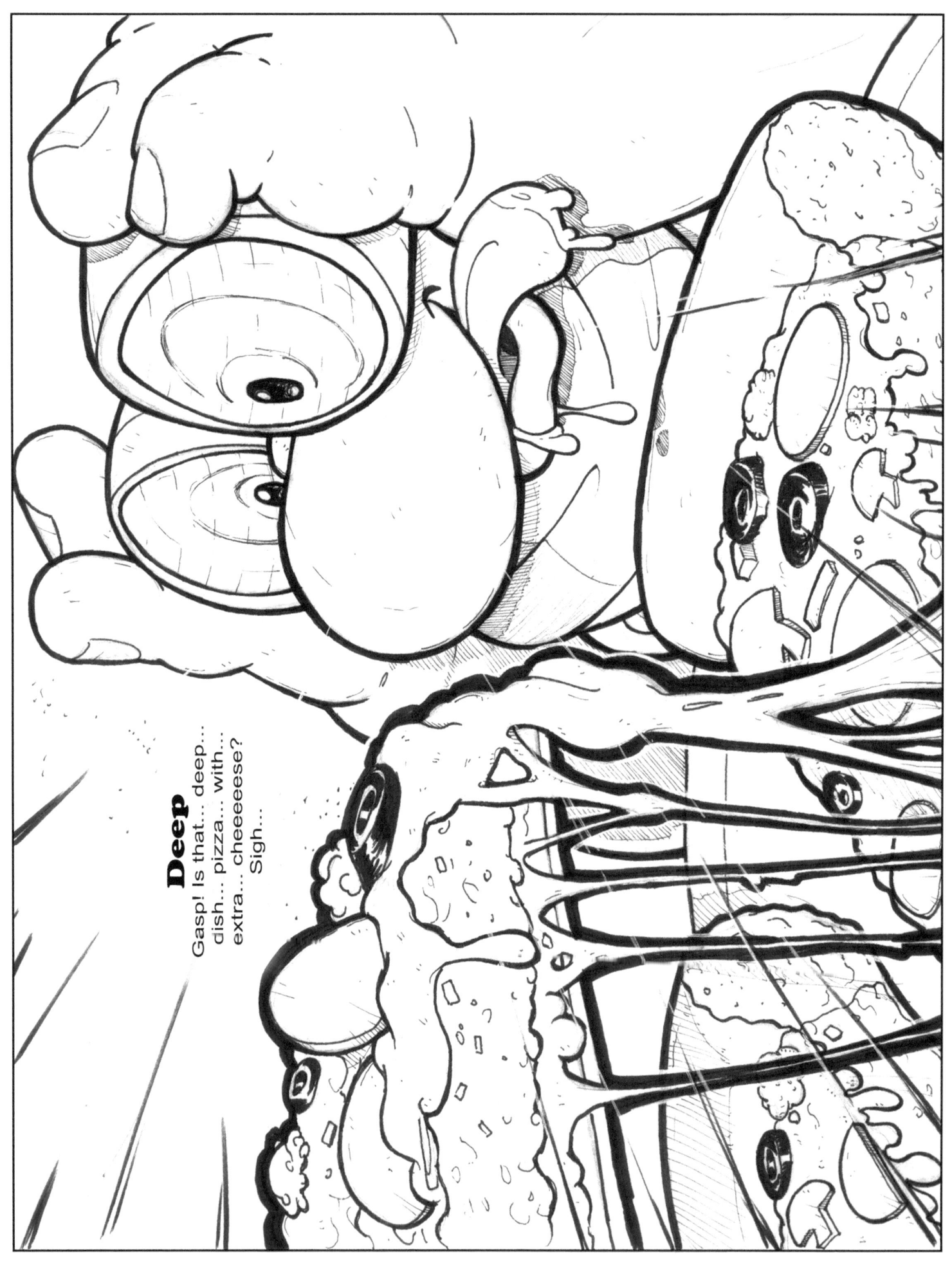

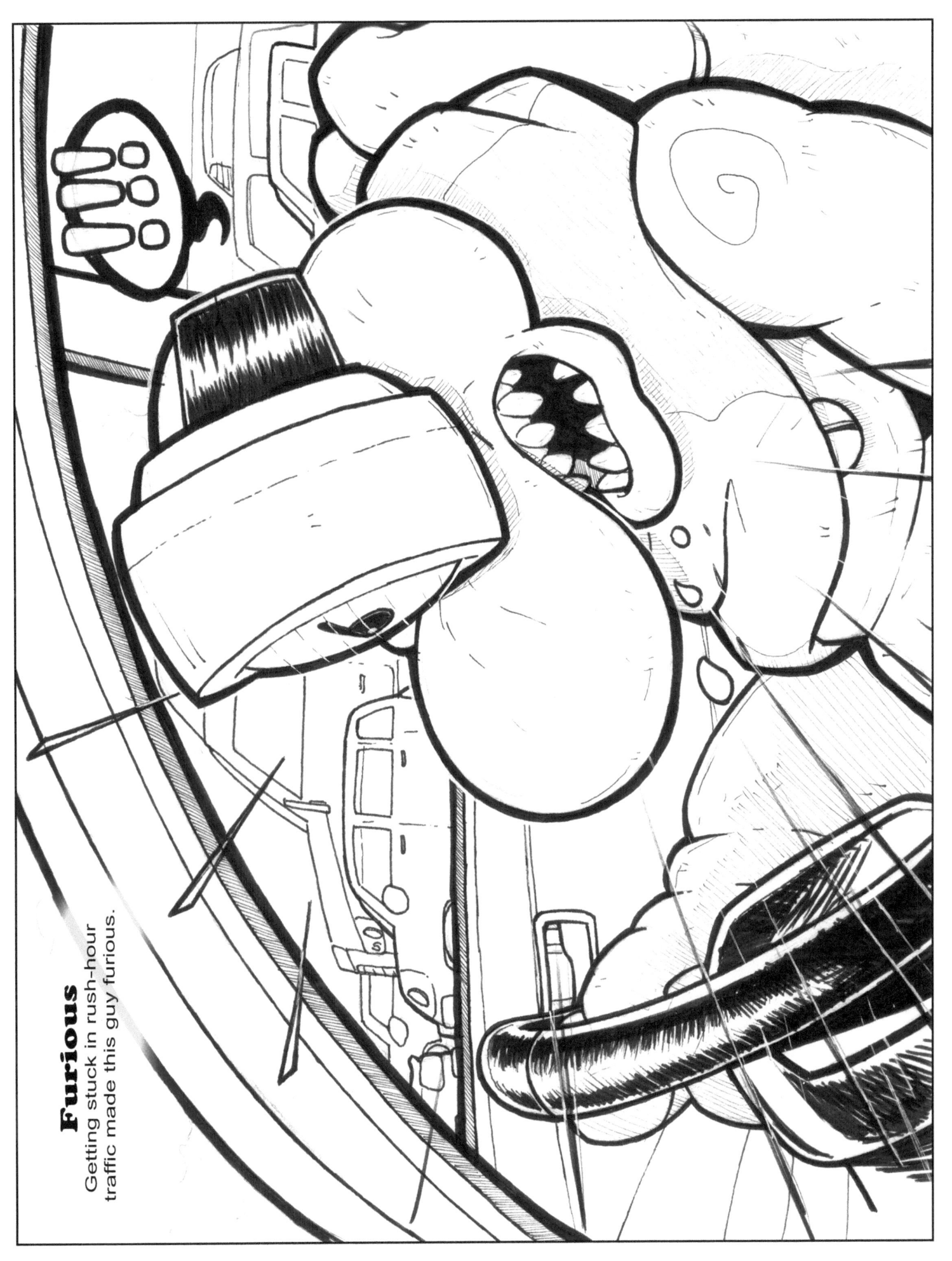

Furious
Getting stuck in rush-hour traffic made this guy furious.

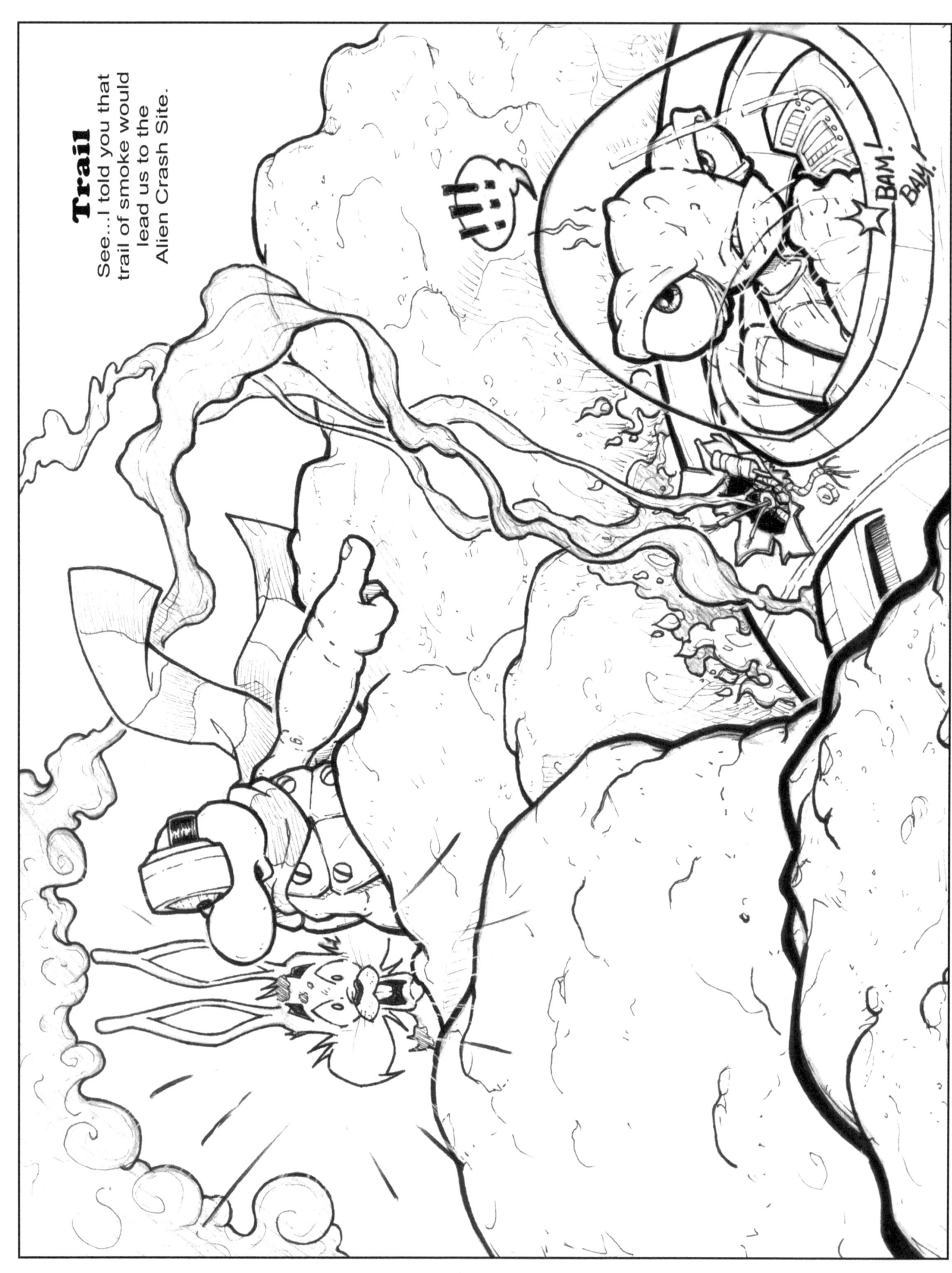

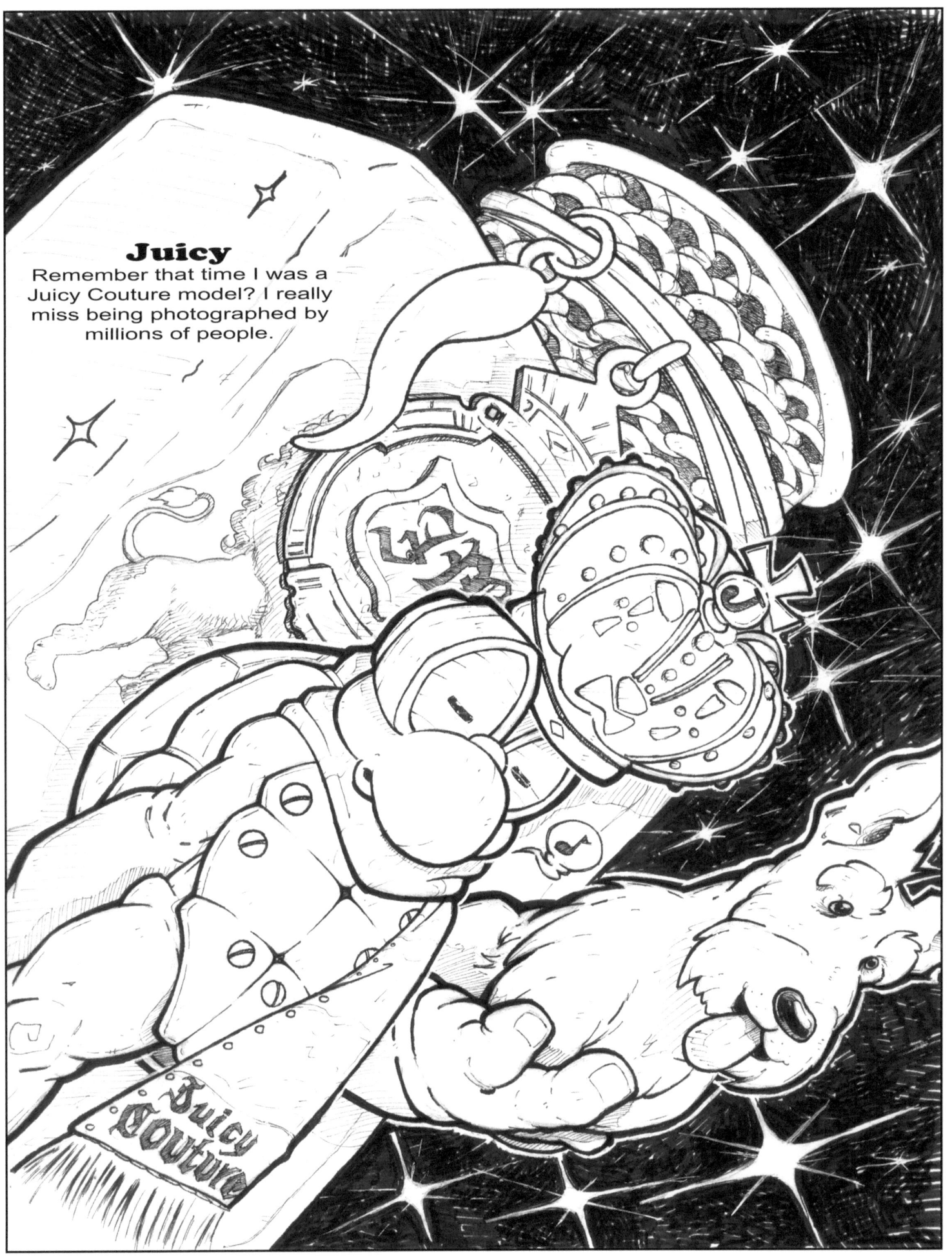

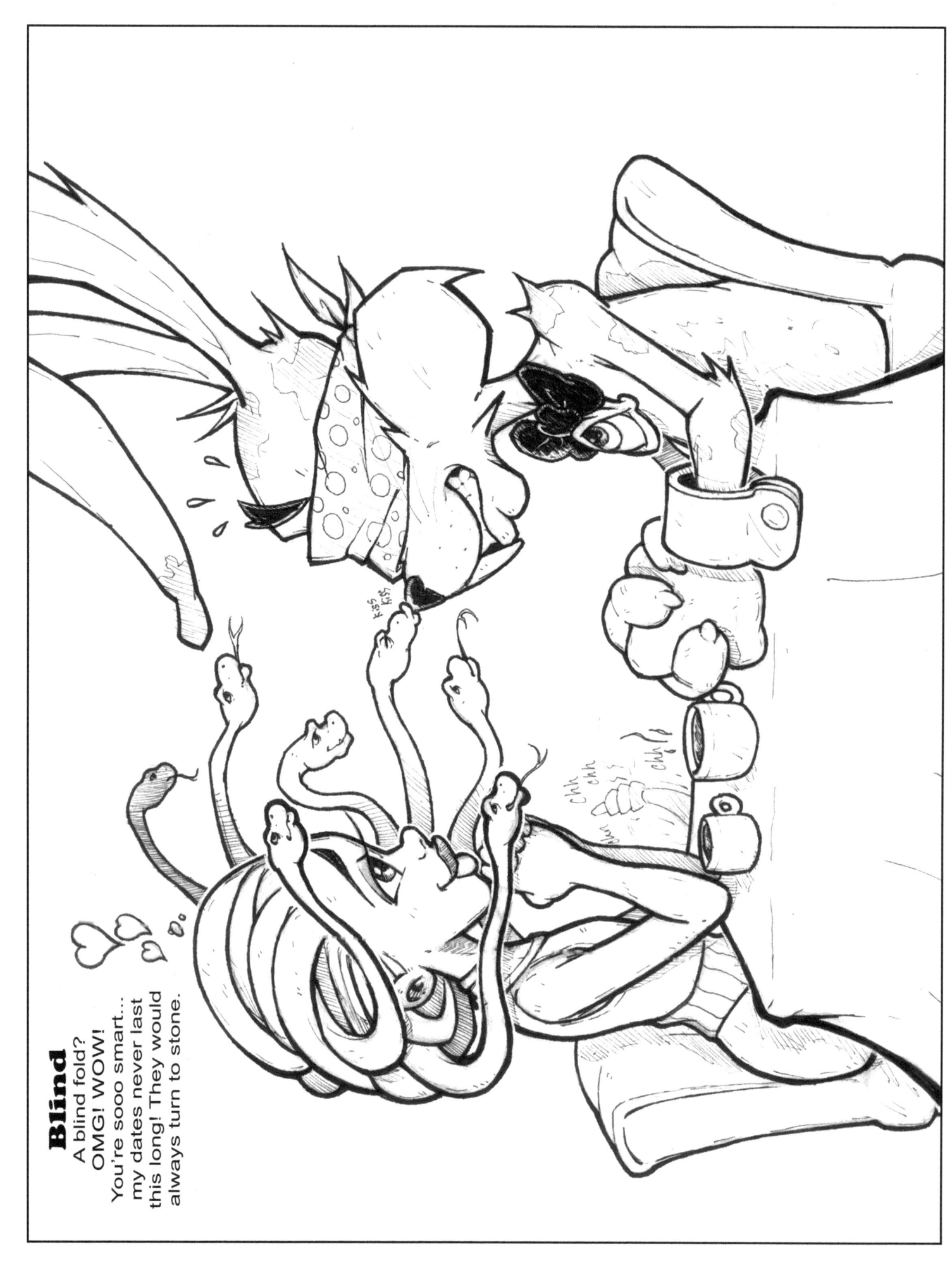

Blind

A blind fold?
OMG! WOW!
You're sooo smart... my dates never last this long! They would always turn to stone.

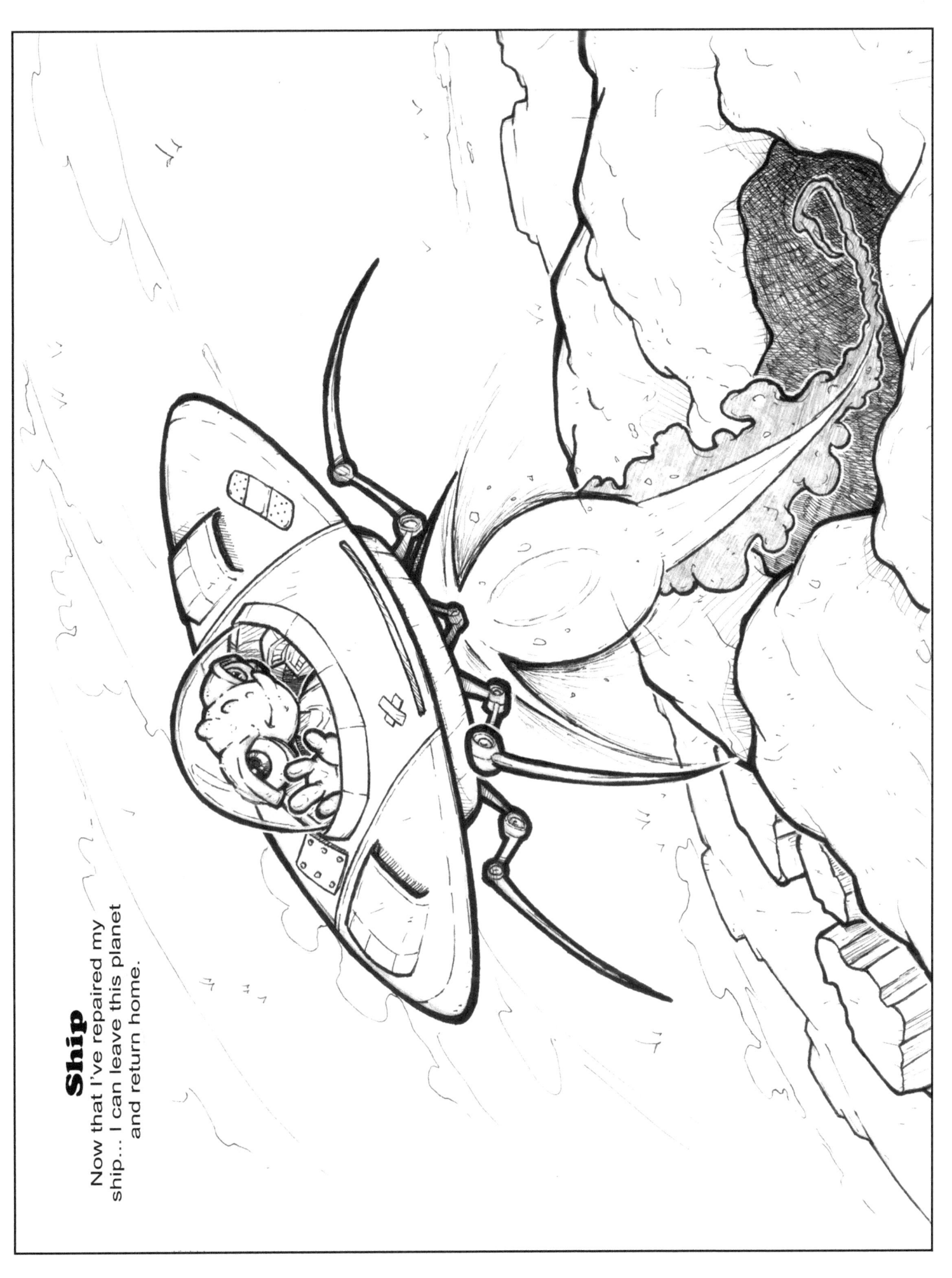

Ship
Now that I've repaired my ship... I can leave this planet and return home.

Squeak

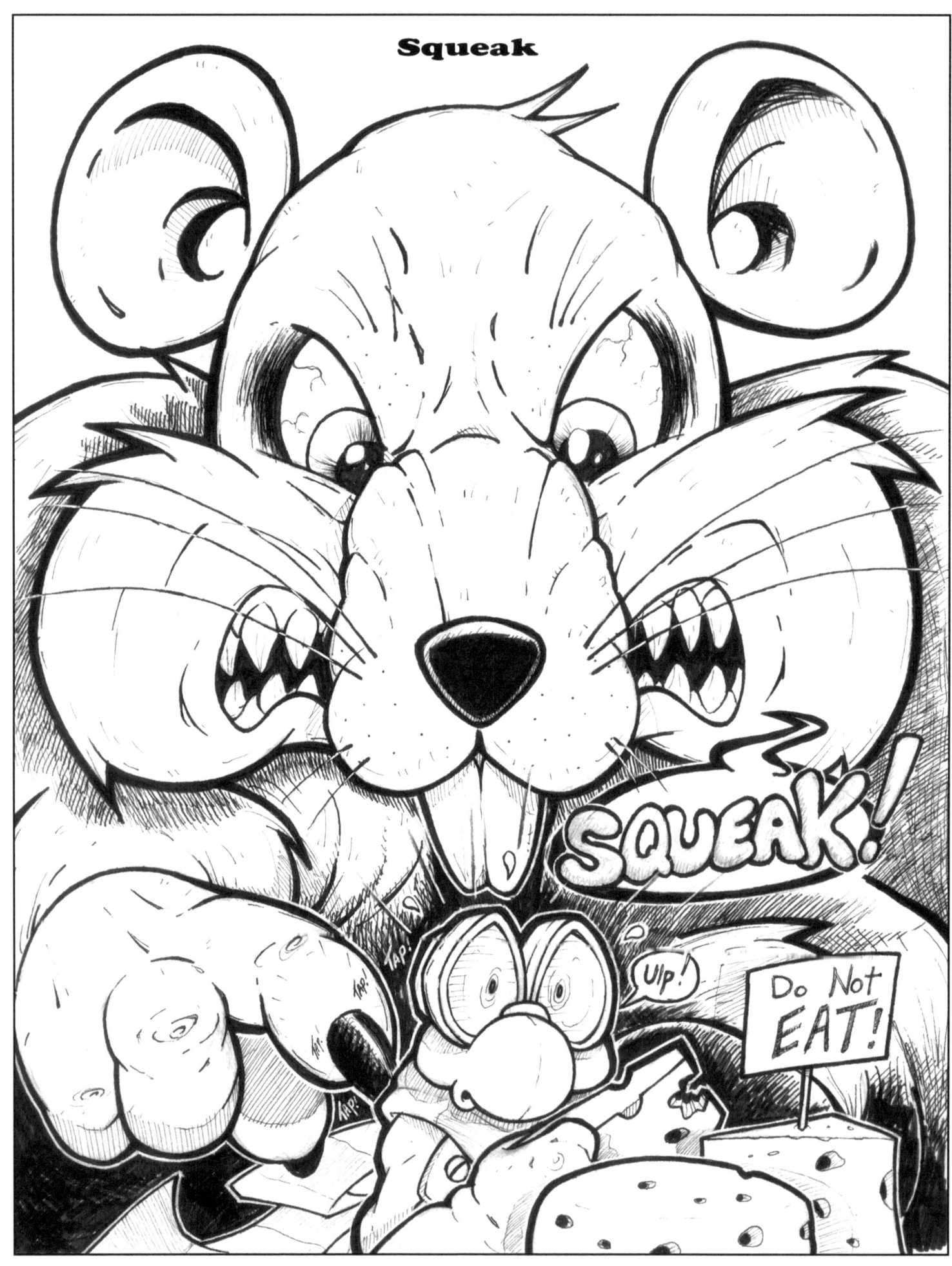

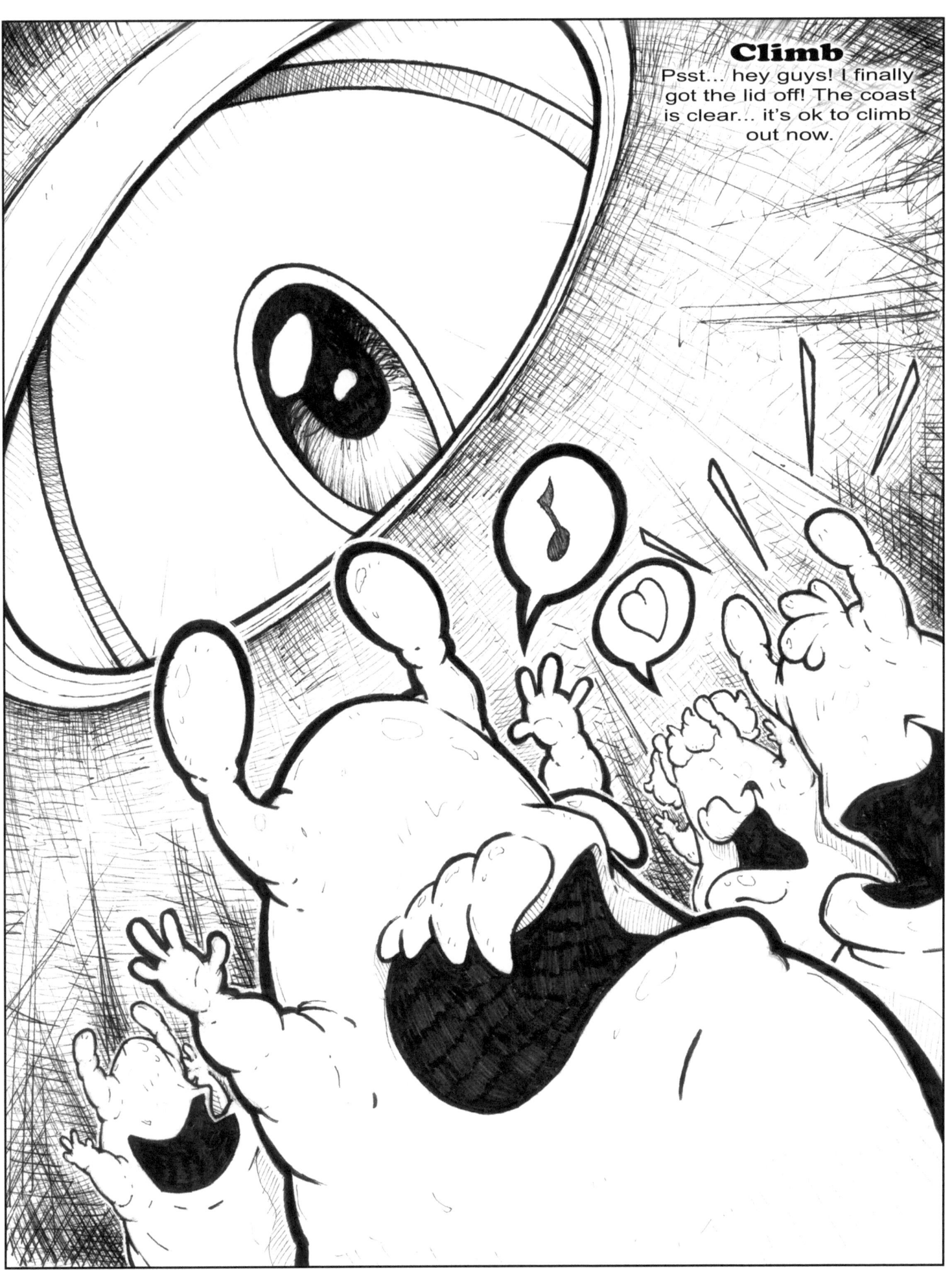

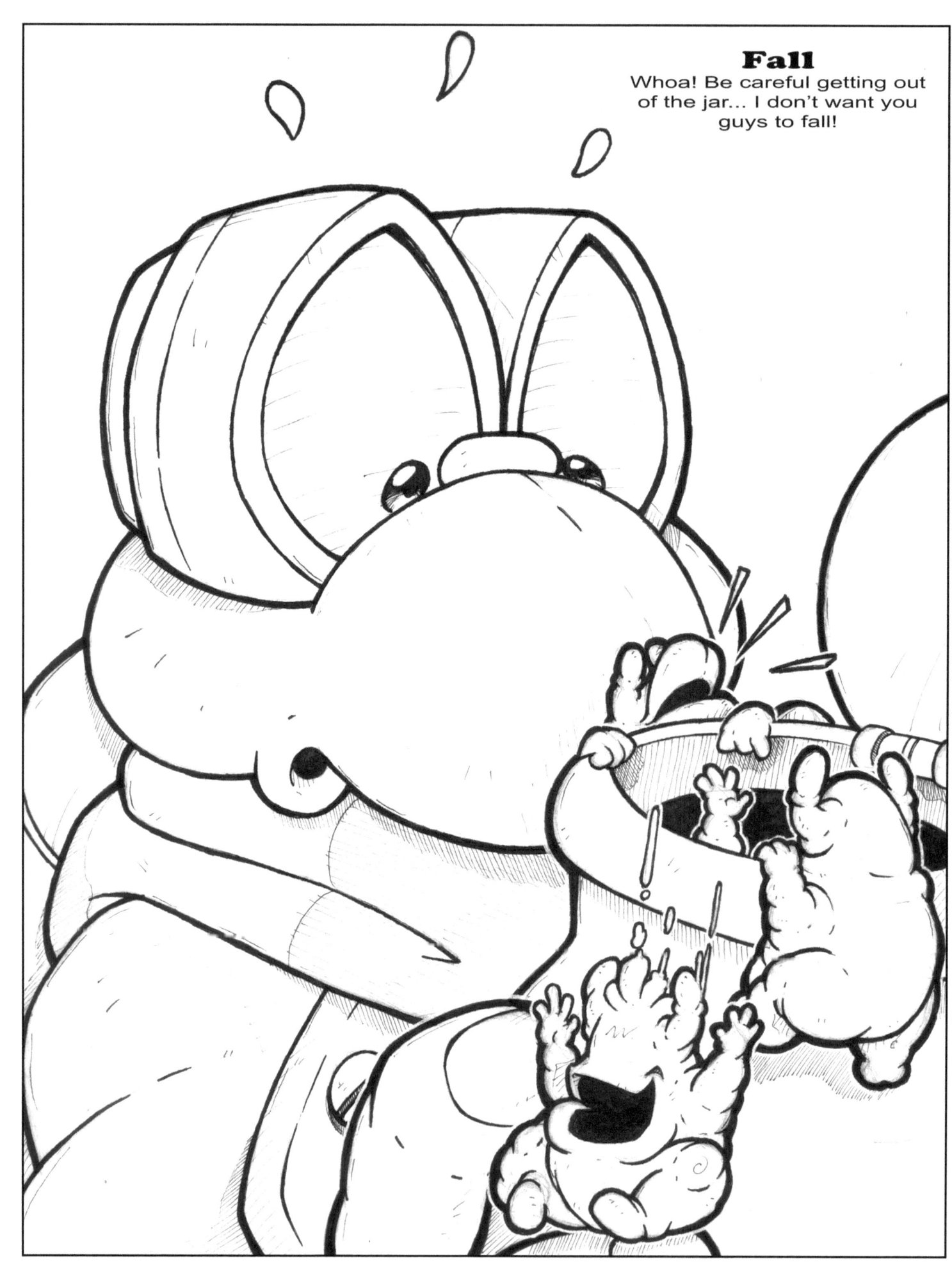

Fall
Whoa! Be careful getting out of the jar... I don't want you guys to fall!

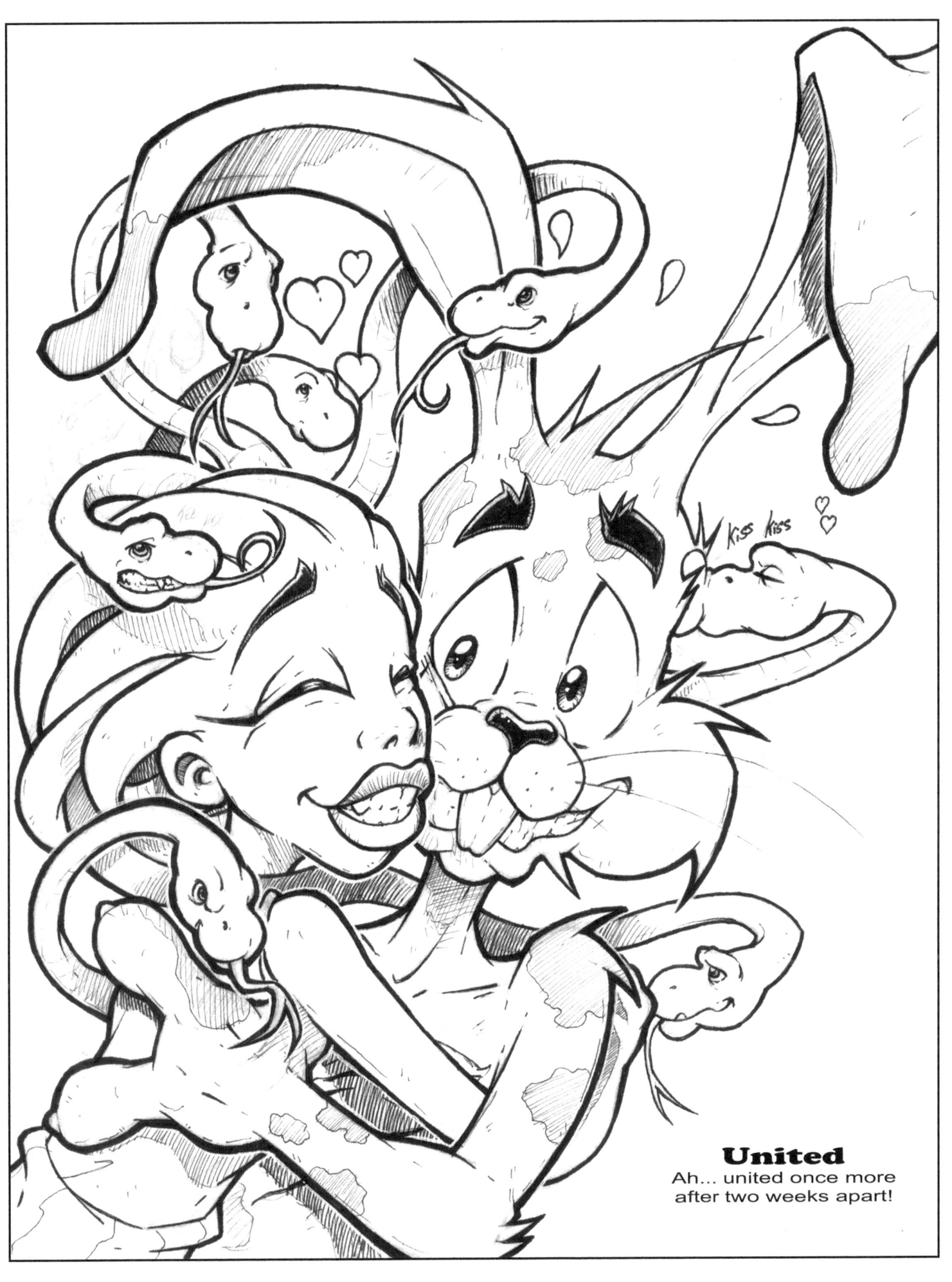

United
Ah... united once more after two weeks apart!

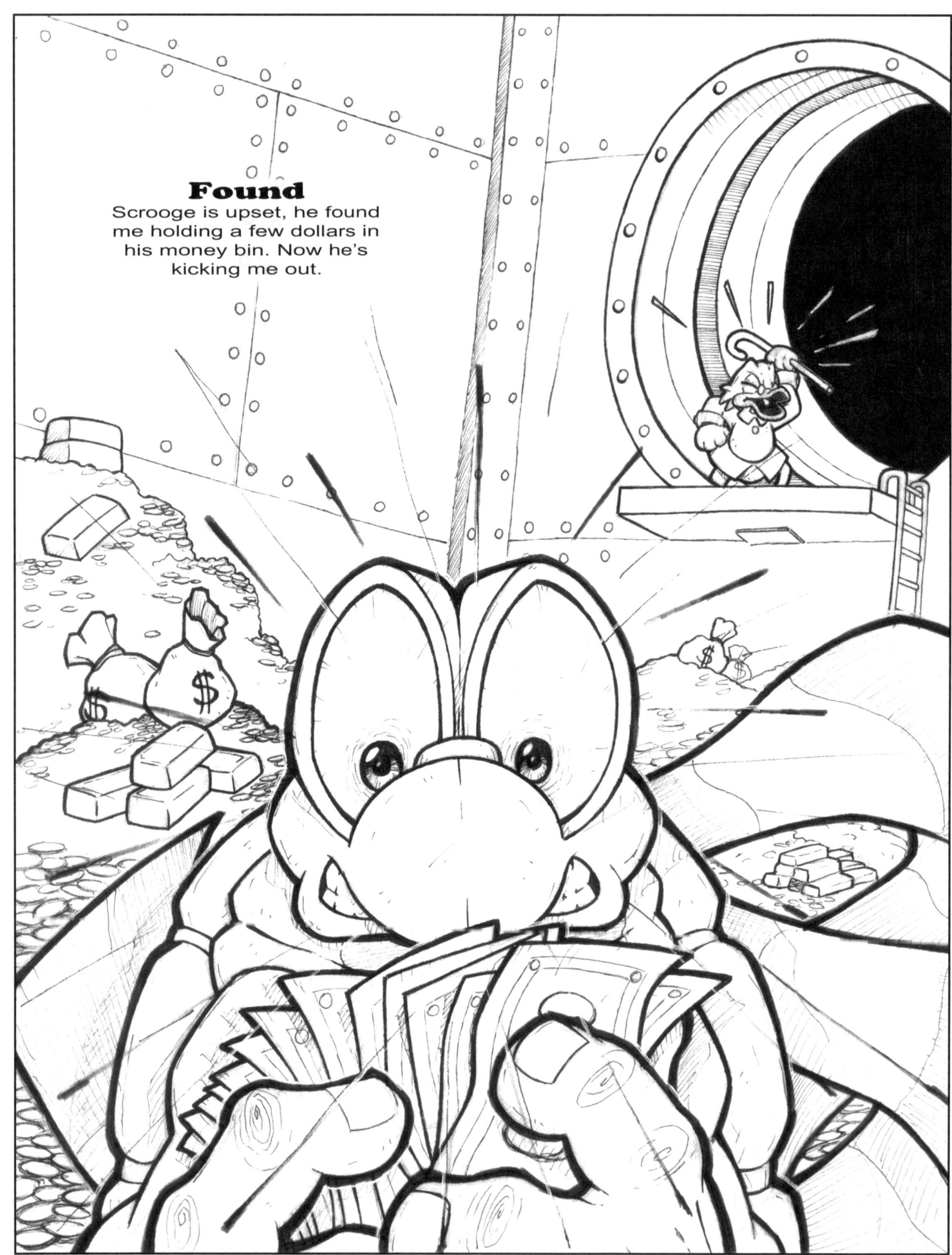

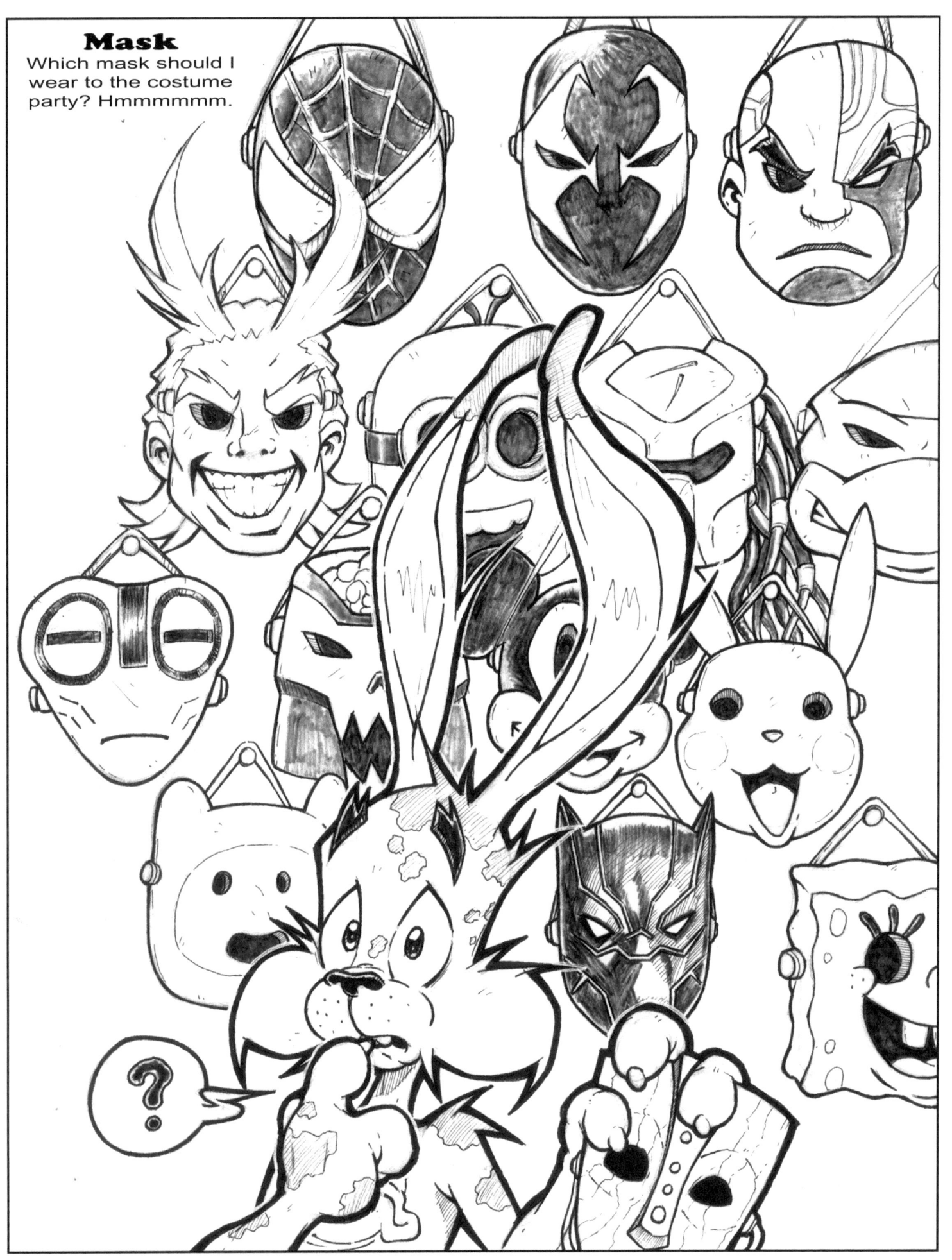

Mask
Which mask should I wear to the costume party? Hmmmmmm.

www.ingramcontent.com/pod-product-compliance
Lightning Source LLC
Chambersburg PA
CBHW051823210526
45473CB00005B/1713